Betty Crocker's
ITALIAN
◆COOKING◆

Betty Crocker's
ITALIAN
·COOKING·

Recipes by
Antonio Cecconi

PRENTICE
HALL
PRESS

NEW YORK ◆ LONDON ◆ TORONTO ◆ SYDNEY ◆ TOKYO ◆ SINGAPORE

PRENTICE HALL PRESS
15 Columbus Circle
New York, NY 10023

PRENTICE HALL PRESS and colophons are registered trademarks
of Simon & Schuster, Inc.

BETTY CROCKER is a registered trademark
of General Mills, Inc.

Library of Congress Cataloging-in-Publication Data

Crocker, Betty.
  [Italian cooking]
  Betty Crocker's Italian cooking.
    p.   cm.
  ISBN 0-13-068263-2
  1. Cookery, Italian.   I. Title.
TX723.C698   1991
641.5945—dc20   89-78153
                                            CIP

Manufactured in the United States of America

10 9 8 7 6 5 4 3 2 1

First Edition

Front Cover: Ravioli with Bolognese Sauce (page 62)

Preceding pages: page i: Doorway in Populonia, Tuscany; page
ii: Seafood Pizza (page 107); page iii: Tuscan countryside

CONTENTS

◆

FOREWORD

◆

Americans have enjoyed Italian cuisine for years. Pizzas, pasta dishes, flavorful tomato sauces and delicious Parmesan, Romano and mozzarella cheeses are all familiar to us, but there is more to the bounty of Italian kitchens. Chef and restaurateur Antonio Cecconi, a native of Sardinia, Italy, has brought his extensive knowledge of Italian cooking to us, and the result is a collection of recipes that are authentic, easy and always delicious.

Italian cooking is not overly complicated or difficult. In fact, you can choose any number of dishes that are easy to make—Farmer's Soup, Steamed Mussels in Wine Sauce, Vermicelli with Fresh Herbs, Angel Hair Pasta in Garlic Sauce—or take advantage of recipes that teach you how to make pizza dough or pasta from scratch. Italians are comfortable using either dried or fresh pasta from the store or homemade pasta, and you, too, can choose which best suits your needs.

The many regions of Italy have produced distinctive dishes that range from the polentas, risottos and cream sauces found in northern Italy to the pizzas, calzones and tomato and olive oil–based dishes found in southern Italy. Seafood from the Mediterranean and Adriatic seas plays an important part in the food of Italy, as do its delicious fruits and vegetables—tomatoes, eggplant, olives, fennel, bell peppers, artichokes, mushrooms, grapes and strawberries.

You will find everything that you need to cook authentic Italian dishes: an introduction that explains Italian regional cuisine and discusses how Italian meals are served; a glossary of terms and recipes for antipasti (appetizers), soups, pasta and sauces, other first courses, pizza and breads, seafood, meats, poultry and game, vegetables and desserts. We have also included menus to help you plan various meals, from a do-ahead meal for a busy day to an elegant seafood-and-fish menu from the Italian Riviera.

Throughout this enticing cookbook, illustrated with mouth-watering photographs, you will find hints, tips and explanations that make these recipes easy to follow. You will also learn about the fascinating history of Italy as it is reflected in its food, as well as enjoy photographs of Italy that will satisfy the armchair traveler in you. With the delicious recipes in this book, you will be able to enjoy the best of Italian cooking, from Chicken Antipasto to Ricotta Cheesecake with Chocolate, right from your own kitchen.

The Betty Crocker Editors

INTRODUCTION

◆

Regions of Italy

Italian food, with its simple preparation and fresh ingredients, has become a familiar part of American cooking. Many people now know Italy as much for its delicious food as for its natural beauty and cultural heritage. Twenty regions compose the Italian mosaic of flavors, ranging from the spicy, Middle Eastern foods of the warm southern islands to the Bavarian-style cuisine of the northern regions high in the Alps.

Olive trees, Populonia, Tuscany

which cheese is added. Chamois, or mountain ram, is the meat specialty of this region and is usually stewed with wine and herbs, accompanied by bread or polenta made from white or yellow cornmeal. Fontina cheese and several types of cured meats such as speck prosciutto are typical of this region. Hot coffee drinks prepared with espresso, grappa brandy and caramelized lemon peel are very popular throughout the many skiing resorts in the area.

Northern Italy

Northern Italy includes the regions of Valle d'Aosta, Piedmont, Lombardy, Veneto, Trentino-Alto Adige, Friuli-Venezia Giulia, Liguria and Emilia-Romagna. Piedmont and Valle d'Aosta border France and Switzerland and are nestled between the Alps and the great Po Valley.

Valle d'Aosta

Valle d'Aosta is entirely mountainous, and its cooking was influenced by the Bavarian-style cuisine of Switzerland, one of its border countries. Peculiar to this region is the absence of pasta and vegetable oils, for which dark oat bread and butter or beef shortening are substituted. Hearty soups are the main staple, prepared with large floating dumplings called *canederli* (German noodles), made of oats or potatoes to

Piedmont

Immediately to the south of Valle d'Aosta spreads the wealthy region of Piedmont, which literally means "at the foot of the mountains." This region is well known for its gastronomic traditions and the vitality of its inhabitants. This agriculturally rich region prides itself on naming, inventing and influencing various styles of cooking that have evolved in other regions of Italy as well as in other countries. This is the home of *fonduta*, known elsewhere as "fondue," and veal and chicken Marengo. Turin, Piedmont's capital, was the seat of the former Italian kings of Savoy, and its cooking reflects the most regal way of preparing breads and pastries. Elaborate sauces and excellent sparkling wines such as Asti Spumante come from this region.

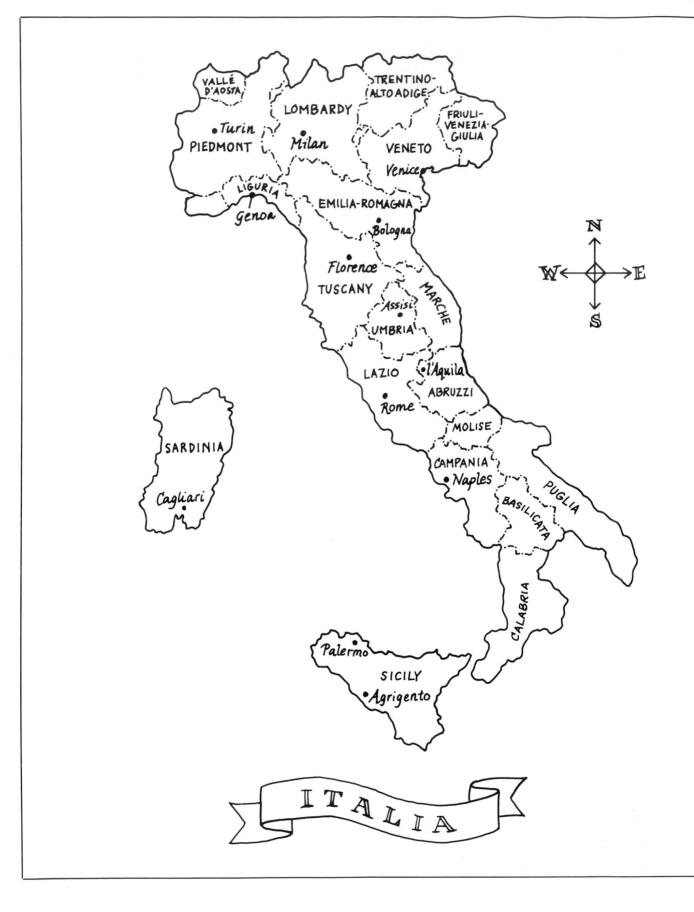

Lombardy

Lombardy is the most affluent Italian region, with a booming economy and prosperous agriculture. Stretching from the Alps in the north to the Po Valley in the south, it is a land of hill towns, ski resorts and peaceful, beautiful lakes. Milan, near the center of Lombardy, is

Gondolas along the Piazza San Marco, Venice

the business capital of Italy; like New York it is something of a melting pot for different cultures and cuisines. Yet Lombard cuisine is easily identifiable from its rich sauces, risottos and polenta dishes, and is renowned for its beef and veal dishes. Some of the cheeses from this region have become world famous, among them Gorgonzola, Parmigiano Grana Padano (the local version of Parmigiano Reggiano), Taleggio and Bel Paese. From this region also comes panettone, the Christmas bread enjoyed by Italian families.

Veneto

Stretching from the great lakes of Lombardy to the shores of the Adriatic Sea is the region of Veneto, which includes Trentino-Alto Adige and Friuli-Venezia Giulia. This area is particularly dear to many who have seen the beauty of its capital, Venice. In the Dolomite Mountains to the north is the enchanting hill town of Verona, where one can sit under a starry sky in the Roman arena and fall under the spell of an opera.

The stunning art of the Veneto region is equally matched by its cuisine. The cooking can be divided into three dominant styles, each from a different province: Veneto (the main province), Friuli (the area bordering Yugoslavia) and the Trentino-Alto Adige (a very independent province, where the customs and language are quite

separate from Italy, resembling those of other Bavarian regions).

The majestic architecture of Venice and its countryside exhibit its importance and power. For centuries Venice was the crossroads for European trading and crusades to the Middle East. The influence of then-exotic spices brought into Italy by merchants is still evident in the use today of saffron in risotto and nutmeg in cream sauces.

Mild weather, an influence of the warm Adriatic Sea, makes the agriculture prosperous, especially around the numerous rivers that flow from the Alps. Fish from fresh waters, lagoons and the sea are fundamental to Venetian cuisine and are frequently prepared with combinations of spices and wine. The lowlands are primarily used for cultivating rice and cornmeal, from which risotto and polenta are made. The use of rice and corn in Veneto overshadow the use of pasta as a staple in the local diet.

The wine and cheeses that come from the mountains and hills near the Alps are highly valued. One can find flavorful cheeses such as Asiago d'Allevo, Mascarpone and Parmesan and wines such as Soave white, Valpolicella, Bardolino and Pinot. Radicchio, now popular in the United States, was first grown in the little town of Treviso, and later, *radicchio di Verona,* a much milder type, was developed here. Under Austrian rule for several decades, Venetian chefs were influenced by the Austrians and created pastries that are quite exuberant and sophisticated, including Christmas *pandoro* and liqueur-laced *fugazza* pastries.

Emilia-Romagna

A combination of two regions, Emilia-Romagna's wonderful cuisine is rooted in two glorious cities:

Parma and Bologna. Both regions have distinctive styles. Emilia is known for its lasagne, tortellini and Parmesan dishes. In Romagna cooks use more fish and olive oil, not as many butter-based sauces. The traditional Bologna hams and the Parmigiano Reggiano cheese have inspired other countries to dupli-

Orvieto in Umbria

cate them, but nothing can match the genuine flavor of the foods manufactured here. Emilia-Romagna exports the world's biggest wheels of Parmesan cheese, meat-stuffed tortellini and prosciutto hams. And it was in Bologna that the classic ragù sauce was invented.

Another specialty of this region are the wines, such as Lambrusco, which complement the region's rich food as they are light, refreshing and have a low alcohol content. Pork and veal are cooked with vegetables and wine, and frequently deep fried. From this practice comes Bologna's nickname, "Grassa"—the fat one. It is only recently that local restaurants have begun to cook with the more healthful olive oil. However, butter remains the base for sauces and desserts.

Liguria

In a crescent between the Alps and the Appennine Mountains and the Mediterranean lies Liguria, forming the beautiful Italian Riviera. The land along the coast is densely cultivated with flowers, herbs and olive and pine groves. The most traditional version of pesto sauce comes from this region.

The warmth of the sea and the protection of the mountains fosters the growth of the high-altitude grapes, which produce robust red wines. Rivaling the culinary splendor of Venice on Italy's other coast is Genoa, the ancient city that was the home

of Christopher Columbus. A seaport for more than 2,000 years, Genoa has influenced many other regions, particularly in the Middle East. It was Genovese sailors who introduced potato and tomato plants to Italy.

Also from its seaside setting comes the rainbow of seafood delicacies that characterize the cuisine of Liguria. Classic dishes include *Cappon magro* (a vegetable and seafood salad), the world-famous Cioppino fish stew and minestrone soup laced with pesto. Another distinctive product of the region is *Farinata pizza,* a pancake-like pizza that originally came from the Orient, prepared by stir-frying pea flour, made from ground dried peas, with tomato sauce and spices. *Focaccia Genovese,* another delicious specialty, is a stuffed pizza.

Central Italy

Central Italy encompasses Tuscany, Umbria, Marche and Lazio and includes Rome and Florence.

Tuscany

Just as Latin was once the language of the Romans and their empire, the Tuscan dialect is considered the proper Italian spoken throughout Italy. A land of pleasant hills and small, refined towns, Tuscany holds many surprises, both cultural and gastronomical. The most brilliant example of its bounty is the capital, Florence, with its stunning Renaissance architecture, art collections and world-famous cuisine. The cuisine of Tuscany is noted for its classic simplicity and the purity of its fresh ingredients. The scents of fresh herbs and other aromas can be an enticing invitation for tourists—a charming introduction to the artistry of Tuscan kitchens.

Herbs such as sage, rosemary, leeks and garlic give a rustic character to the food and are usually incorporated in the main portion of the dish rather than in the sauce. Pasta dishes are not a mainstay of Tuscan cuisine; those that are served have unpretentious, flavorful sauces. Instead, rice is common.

Trees line the road in Baratti, Tuscany

Much of the simple, modest Tuscan cuisine has influenced the French and the English. Sometimes one even finds such terms as *béchamel* (from the Italian *Balsa Mella*) and *pâte à choux* (from the Italian *Pasta Calda*) appearing in their original Italian on restaurant menus in other countries as a nod to their Tuscan heritage.

Tuscany offers a substantial variety of foods such as *Tortelli di Zucca* (Pumpkin-filled Ravioli), spit-roasted meats with little fat used in their cooking, exotic Crisp Fried Zucchini Flowers, dozens of fresh-cooked vegetables and crunchy desserts frequently made with a variety of nuts.

Tuscany is famous for its wines, many of which have won prizes around the world. Foremost is the Chianti, from a district of only thirty square miles. In Tuscany, olive trees mingle with the grapevines; both are intrinsically linked to Tuscany's economy and cuisine.

Workers at medieval castles and villas continue planting and harvesting grapes and olives as they have for centuries, but modern technology has made some inroads. The combination of ancient agricultural methods with detailed attention to the planting—and new innovations such as mechanical harvesting—provides quality exports of wines and olive oils known throughout the world.

Wines are incorporated in several desserts and fruitcakes, and these sweets are usually eaten on separate occasions, rather than served as part of a regular meal. This is particularly true for the delicious nut-based cakes and breads, which, when accompanied by a glass of strong *Vinsanto* (holy dessert wine), can be particularly luscious.

Umbria

Small in size, Umbria is the only region in the Italian peninsula not bordered by the sea. It is tucked between Lazio and Marche, with small cities scattered through its many mountains. The food found in Perugia, Assisi and Spoleto rivals the arts, opera, crafts and architecture that make these towns famous.

While Umbria doesn't have seafood, mountain streams provide tasty trout and carp, which are marinated and cooked with fresh herbs, notably marjoram. Traditional pasta dishes are prepared, baked and then served as timbales, which are sliced and often served cold. Mountain mushrooms such as *porcini* and *tartufi* are the main ingredients of Umbrian pies, which gives them exquisite flavor and a lovely appearance. Producing tantalizing wine such as Orvieto and liqueurs is an ancient tradition of the numerous monasteries of the region. Wild boar and aged mountain beef are also renowned.

Marche

Marche, on the mid-Adriatic coast, is one of the most appealing but lesser known regions of the entire peninsula. Its four major cities, almost overlooking one another, sit atop the pleasant

Appennine foothills, with Ancona, its capital, facing the Adriatic shore from high cliffs. The reliably mild climate is reflected in the cuisine, where subtle spicing is the norm and seafood stews are common. From Marche departs one of the largest fishing fleets of the country, which consistently provides the local

Umbrian landscape

markets with an abundant selection of fresh fish. In the countryside towns of Urbino, Recanati and Pesaro, cattle and hogs have been raised since the days of the Renaissance. This is reflected in the role that cured meats such as salami and prosciutto play in its cuisine.

A giant type of green olive grown in the area of Ascoli Piceno becomes a delicacy when filled with Parmesan, ground meats, eggs and spices, and then deep-fried; this treat is found in no other region of Italy. Peaches and apples are the predominant fruits grown in Marche. Also noteworthy is the white truffle found during the fall months. Particularly renowned is the sauce known as *salsa del Duca D'Urbino,* similar to English Worcestershire sauce. In fact, a local legend has it that after the Duke of Urbino lost a medieval battle, he had to surrender his recipe to the Saxon victor, which explains how the sauce traveled to England.

Lazio

Lazio is known for its capital—Rome. It has a simple cuisine similar to Tuscany's. Pasta is favored, especially *bucatini* and *penne.* Rome was the birthplace of *spaghetti carbonara,* and outside of Naples is the best place to eat pizza, baked in its traditional form with wood fires. Toppings are simple; sometimes just one is used, and it can be one of many vegetables, such as tomatoes, zucchini and mushrooms.

Southern Italy

Southern Italy is composed of Abruzzi, Molise, Campania, Puglia, Basilicata and Calabria, with Naples its major city.

Abruzzi

Abruzzi is a region of rugged mountains, sunny plateaus and a rocky seacoast bordering the Adriatic Sea. Sparsely populated, the region is primarily agricultural. Some of the finest pastas come from Fara San Martino—due to excellent wheat grown in the region—and are a prime source of exports to other countries. Olive oils are also of excellent quality and are commonly used for deep-frying the seafood that come from the coastal waters.

Molise

Smaller than Abruzzi, Molise is in many ways similar in both cuisine and geography. Campobasso is the main city of Molise; fresh seafood and short-cut pasta, made from soft wheat and served with hot pepper and tomato sauce, dominate the cuisine. Lamb and baby goat are traditionally served in most restaurants and are usually spit-roasted. Seafood appetizers are also a specialty of this region, served simply with olive oil and lemon.

Campania

Campania is one of the most fascinating and complex regions of Italy, with densely populated cities, a beautiful coast and ancient ruins. Blessed by the Mediterranean sun most of the year, the great valley around Naples is shaded by the ever-towering volcano Vesuvius, and its rich volcanic ash makes the region the most fertile in the world for cultivating tomatoes. Similar to California in climate, it produces an overwhelming array of vegetables still grown in small family plots—without pesticides.

From this bounty a local cuisine has evolved that uses many spices and has created flavor combinations that are famous throughout Italy.

Campania also produces fresh mozzarella cheese, which is made from the milk of a local breed of water buffalo. Seafood from coastal waters makes up

Detail of a balustrade and grape arbor, Sovrano, Lazio

more than half of the food consumed in the region. Pizza was invented in Naples by creative housewives, providing a use for the newly imported tomatoes (originally they were mysterious newcomers used only as ornamental plants).

Puglia

Puglia is the "heel" of the Italian boot, a long strip of land that forms its own peninsula. Italians regard it as the vegetable garden of the country, where the freshest greens, seafood and light meats provide a dazzling combination. Foods are generously basted, fried, marinated or drizzled with olive oil, which is the staple of all the local recipes.

It is interesting to note that this is the region from which most boats come and go to Greece, Turkey and most other Middle Eastern countries. The interchange of traffic dates back to pre-Roman times, and it is no surprise to see Egyptian or Arab foods at the heart of this region, such as fava beans, lentils and sweet-and-sour ratatouille salads; lamb, rabbit and chicken acquire an exotic tang from the cumin, hot pepper and saffron that season them. Another interesting tradition is a tomato and horsemeat stew slowly cooked in clay pots over hot coals.

These Oriental hints are also found in the sweets, prepared mainly with honey and nuts. A curiously sweet, fresh cheese (considered a des-

sert) is the Manteca, which is an apple-size fresh cheese with sweet butter in the center. It is accompanied by large homemade loaves of crusty bread. Often the bread is imprinted with a family seal because bread is brought by the local housewives to their neighborhood baker to be baked, and it is later identified by its seal. *Calzoni* and *panzarotti* foldovers of this region are prepared in two versions, sweet or savory, and in contrast with the Neapolitan version, are deep-fried rather than baked.

Basilicata

Flanked by Calabria on the west and Apulia on the east, Basilicata is a small region with ancient culinary traditions. Both neighboring regions influence its cooking, and here again there is a hint of exotic spices. Because it is at the center of the Ionic gulf, seafood plays a major role as do olive oil and tomatoes. Strong goat cheese—dark and chewy, with a pleasant stringiness—is made in the shape of animals; the shapes vary from one little town to the next, so locals can tell the origin of the cheese just from its shape. In the district of Lucania, legend has it that the Roman garrisons used to demand provisions from the people of Lucania in the form of a special mix of ground and spiced meats that had a very long shelf life—the precursor of modern sausages.

Calabria

Calabria, right at the "toe" of Italy, shares the Oriental heritage of Sicily, colonized first by the Greeks, then by the Arabs. It is one of the few regions where hot peppers are commonly used. As in Apulia, lamb, game and seafood play a major role in the diet. *Capozello* and *cervellata* (head meat) are important meat dishes. Very hard wheat also provides excellent short-cut pasta, which is frequently prepared with special vegetables. Eggplant is the most prized vegetable and is used liberally as an appetizer, first course or main dish. It is spread on bread as *Melanzane a Scapece* (pickled eggplant). Some of Calabria's robust red wines are also noteworthy.

Sardinian coastline, near Santa Margherita

Italian Islands

Italy's two islands, Sicily and Sardinia, offer a wide range of attractions from their distinctive cuisines to their scenic coastlines.

Sicily

The southernmost Italian region, the island of Sicily, has seen many different cultures. Phoenicians, followed by Greeks, Romans, Normans, Spaniards and Arabs all colonized Sicily. It became part of Italy in the middle of the nineteenth century and has preserved a little of each of these cultures. Couscous, saffron rice, eggplant and olive dishes, seafood and desserts can also be found in several other Mediterranean countries. With its sunny, warm weather most of the year, Sicily has always attracted tourists as well as settlers. Over the past fifty years, modern industry has revolutionized outdated irrigation systems, projecting Sicily into full-scale export of citrus fruits, grapes and vegetables.

Wines and the business of fishing are also important to the economy of the island and rival those of the otherwise much more sophisticated northern Italian regions. Desserts from Palermo and Catania such as cannoli pastries, cassata cakes and ices are known worldwide. Typical pasta dishes have sea-food and hot peppers featured in their sauces, and tangy olives are present in many dishes.

Sardinia

Sardinia is Italy's second largest island. The combination of rugged mountains and a spectacular coastline accounts for its popularity with tourists. Though invaded and colonized over the centuries by the Spanish and others, Sardinia has preserved its independent culture, language and gastronomy. The pride of its inhabitants is reflected in its cuisine, which has achieved a well-defined identity.

The staples of the Sardinian cuisine are fish, lamb and hard-wheat pastas. Shellfish is served as an appetizer and fish is grilled, fried or served with succulent tomato and wine sauces. Sardinia grows excellent durum wheat, from which semolina is produced, and it is used to prepare unusual pasta dishes such as ravioli filled with spinach or ricotta cheese and nuts, a type of porridge with lentils and tomato sauce, and tiny gnocchi, much smaller in size than the ones of the mainland.

From the island's interior come suckling pigs, boar and game; these are usually cooked on open-flame grills and flavored with fragrant herbs such as wild fennel, myrtle, rosemary, bay leaves, basil and saffron, all of which grow wild on the island. Pecorino Romano, a pungent cheese, is made from goat milk. Vegetables are fewer than on the mainland due to frequent droughts, but are quite flavorful. Some very strong local wines and Sassari olive oil have won national attention and are frequently used for cooking.

Desserts are simple and usually include honey and nuts; traditionally desserts are only eaten on special occasions, and sugary desserts have a special role at weddings, funerals and baptisms.

Flavors and Spices

Many of the flavors, scents and spices associated with Italian cooking are familiar to Americans. The tomato, of course, has become something of a symbol for Italian cooking—sliced fresh with basil, cooked to make sauces, sun-dried for soups, pizza, pasta or long-term storage. The spices most commonly used to enhance the flavor of the tomato are basil and oregano, often paired with garlic and onion. These spices are essential to many Italian sauces, particularly in southern Italy.

In the north, olive oil and tomatoes give way to butter and cream sauces, with more subtle and exotic flavors. Spices were introduced in the Middle Ages by Venetian merchants, and their use slowly spread throughout the country. Foods that would otherwise have spoiled before the days of refrigeration were spiced with pepper to retard spoilage or hide the flavor of spoilage. Today, salt and pepper are still the basic ingredients used to cure meat. Cinnamon, cloves, nutmeg and other Oriental spices—once a luxury of the wealthy—slowly became available to cooks in humbler kitchens as the transportation and storage of spices improved. These spices are still used in many meat dishes and desserts, especially in the northern regions.

In southern Italy, the sunny climate fosters the cultivation of caper bushes, bay leaves, rosemary, basil and thyme, which, along with a hint of hot pepper, spice meats and seafoods. Italian food isn't spiced to be burning hot; if hot peppers are called for in a dish, only the pulp is used, which is not as hot as its seeds and inner core. Citron, or candied fruit, is used in the breads and sweets of northern Italy, while nuts, cinnamon and raisins are more commonly used in the south.

Substitutions in Cooking

Fresh herbs are preferable to dry herbs, but when they just aren't available, you can substitute 1 teaspoon of dried herbs for 3 tablespoons of fresh. Throughout these recipes, authentic Italian ingredients are used. Sometimes you may need to substitute ingredients, and you can use the following guidelines. For imported black olives (sometimes called Kalamata olives) you can substitute Greek olives or domestic ripe olives; for pear-shaped tomatoes or imported pear-shaped tomatoes you can substitute regular tomatoes. Also look for canned domestic tomatoes labeled "Italian-style." When a recipe calls for extra-virgin olive oil, you should use the best quality olive oil available, as it is an important component of the recipe.

The Influence of Italian Cuisine

Legend has it that the Chinese invented the noodle, and the Italians learned this art when Marco Polo returned from his travels to China. He also imported to his native Venice the silkworm and spices of the Orient. Some say it might have been the other way around, that this keen explorer was retracing ancient trading routes described in Roman texts and that Italy actually did invent the noodle. In any case, noodles are now an integral part of Italian cuisine, and Italian pasta dishes are world famous.

Another well-publicized Italian explorer was Christopher Columbus. We all know about his "discovery" of America. During the first centuries after the discovery of the New World, several new foods were brought to Italy, among them herbs, vegetables and fruits. When the tomato was first brought to Europe it was considered an ornamental plant. It was only after hungry Italians, ravaged by famine, started cooking with tomatoes—drying them in the sun and storing them in paste form—that other countries began using them as food. A classic example of how the tomato influenced other cuisines is the Spanish paella, a dish that became a favorite of most other Latin countries, in which a harmonious blend of tomatoes and saffron marries chicken and seafood.

During medieval times aristocratic European families were fascinated by the Italian Renaissance, with its beautiful art and bustling industry. Many aristocrats from other countries married Italians who brought entire entourages with them to their new homes to re-create the ambience of Italy, so far away. Most important, they reproduced their "home cooking." This is how Italian ices were introduced to northern Europe and how the *balsamella* sauce became "béchamel" and Genovese cake, "genoise." The British were inspired by the sweetness of Marsala wine and converted it to sherry, and when Florentine bankers opened trading offices in London, the *bistecca,* popular in Florence, became "beef steak." In the nineteenth century, immigrants from southern Italy headed for the Americas, and pasta and pizza became part of the North American diet. Immigrants to South America brought Parmesan cheese and cured meats to the cuisine of their new country.

Italian Diet

Italians have been taking food seriously for more than 2,000 years, and it is amazing to note that most of the food eaten in Italy today remains roughly the same. Many people find the basic Italian diet—with its emphasis on olive oil, not butter; pasta, polenta and risotto dishes; sensible portions and only occasional use of desserts—to be one of the most healthful ways to eat.

Roman legions were fed *garum,* the precursor of pizza topping, which was a cured fish spread placed on top of flat bread and moistened by olive oil. This diet seems to have had great merit since these legions conquered one country after another to form the mighty Roman Empire.

Italians respect regular mealtimes; the family gathers at the table every day, not just on special occasions. Instead of concentrating on one main dish flanked by side dishes, their meals consist of a series of courses served and eaten separately. This allows more time to talk and enjoy the meal and aids the digestion.

The variety of foods offered is frequently served on a sampling basis—small tastes of several dishes. Unfortunately it is impossible for most Americans to go home for lunch, but in Italy the main course of the day is served at lunch, which is frequently followed by a siesta, in order to be re-energized for the rest of the day. Of course, Italians work later to recover the time, and dinner is usually served around nine o'clock. The Mediterranean dinner is a scaled-down version of their lunch, eaten during the late evening hours. It also is an occasion for families to come together at the end of the day, relax and enjoy in one another's company.

A typical menu gives us insight into the Italian diet. Large meals begin with a light *antipasto,* literally "before the pasta," that stimulates the appetite for the first course. These antipasti are generally light, cured meats or fresh seafood. Olive oil and tangy lemon juice or vinegar highlight the food's flavor.

Next is the first course, or *primo.* Not necessarily pasta, it can be soup, risotto, polenta, or gnocchi. The first course is enjoyed in its own right, served in small portions to prevent overwhelming the other courses.

The second course, or *secondo,* is the main portion of the meal and is usually a meat, seafood or poultry dish. White meat is generally preferred to red, olive oil in place of other fats and fresh herbs are used rather than a great deal of salt.

To complement the main dish a *contorno* is served, which is either a salad or a raw or cooked vegetable, prepared simply. The purpose of this dish is to cleanse the palate, so heavy sauces or dressings are rare. The vegetables lead to the end of the meal, which can be either cheese with crusty bread or fresh fruit, though rarely a very sweet pastry. Some people drink espresso coffee as a "digestive" after a meal, though it is more commonly served for breakfast with a roll.

While Italians have created luscious desserts known the world over, these are usually served only on special occasions. Italians serve dessert as a separate event, over which to socialize or celebrate, not as part of a meal. Sweets are generally served with coffee or a glass of wine.

Following pages: Herbs and Cheeses Frequently Used in Italian Cooking: (1) Romano (2) Italian Parsley (3) Parmesan (4) Ricotta (5) Mint (6) Basil (7) Watercress (8) Thyme (9) Rosemary (10) Provolone (11) Fontina (12) Asiago (13) Sage (14) Mozzarella (15) Gorgonzola (16) Swiss (17) Bel Paese (18) Oregano (19) Mascarpone (20) Marjoram

GLOSSARY

◆

Alchermes: A strong cherry liqueur.

Amaretti: Derived from the term *amaro* (bitter), these traditional bittersweet cookies are prepared with equal amounts of bitter almonds (usually apricot kernels) and regular almonds.

Anchovies: Small fish common in the Mediterranean Sea, eaten fresh or as fillets cured in oil or salt. Popular in salads and sauces.

Antipasti: "Before the pasta" is the literal translation. Antipasti can be any number of appetizers, usually cold, that are served before a meal.

Arborio Rice: Large, unhulled rice grains used to make risotto dishes.

Asti Spumante: A bubbly white wine with a low alcohol content, similar to champagne, from the Asti region in Piedmont. It is generally used for holidays and special occasions.

Balsamic Vinegar: A sweet-sour vinegar made from white grapes and aged for several years in wooden barrels.

Bel Paese: Literally translated, this means "nice country" and is a soft cow's milk cheese from Lombardy.

Bolognese Sauce: A traditional meat sauce from Bologna, prepared with wine, tomatoes and meats such as beef, veal and pork.

Bruschette: Toasted bread slices topped with garlic and olive oil.

Bucatini: A long, hollow noodle, thicker than spaghetti, that originated in Naples.

Cacciatore: This word means "hunter" and is used to describe several meat and game dishes in which olives, wine and mushrooms are cooked with meat. These were the simple ingredients hunters had on hand to turn their catch into an easy meal.

Calamari: A type of small squid that is cut into rings or strips and deep fried. Sometimes it is also served in its own ink juices in the form of a stew.

Calzone: A foldover pizza stuffed with cheese, or cheese and meat. The Italian name means "stuffed stocking," which a calzone resembles after it is baked or deep fried.

Cannelloni: A large, 4-inch-long, tubular noodle, usually stuffed and baked.

Cannoli: A tubular pastry shell that is baked and filled with a sweetened ricotta cheese and candied fruit-cream mixture. Originally from Sicily.

Capellini: One of the thinnest cut spaghetti noodles, served with light sauces. It is a very quick pasta to prepare as it needs to boil only a few minutes.

Capers: The bud from a caper bush, often used in sauces and salads as a piquant seasoning. The buds are harvested and pickled in brine.

Carbonara: A Roman pasta dish made with a sauce of eggs, garlic and bacon. It was popularized by the Allied Forces who liberated Rome in World War II; they found the dish reminiscent of bacon and egg breakfasts. The name means "coal miner," after the miners who were credited with inventing the dish.

Carne: The Italian word for "meat," *carne* refers to all kinds of meat.

Cherry Liqueur: *See* alchermes.

Chianti: One of the best-known red Italian wines that comes from the Chianti district near Florence. It is excellent with meat dishes.

Crema: This translates as "cream," and it can be used to describe sweet desserts or thick, creamy soups.

Crostini: Sliced and toasted Italian bread used as an appetizer and in soups.

Ditalini: A pasta cut into short segments that look like "thimbles." Typically it is cooked in soups or served with a vegetable sauce.

Farfalle: A butterfly-shaped pasta.

Fennel: The bulb at the base of the fennel plant has a refreshing licorice-like flavor, excellent raw or cooked. The green bushy top, similar to dill weed, can be used to season soups and stews or as a garnish.

Fennel Seeds: The seeds of the fennel plant are used as a spice for meats and sauces. Like the bulb of the plant, they have a licorice-like flavor.

Fettuccine: Literally meaning "little strands," fettuccine is a long, flat noodle, roughly 1/4 inch wide.

Focaccia: Either a flat loaf of bread or a leavened, seasoned and filled dough that resembles a stuffed pie.

Fontina: A semisoft cow's milk cheese from northern Italy that is ideal for fondues.

Frittata: The Italian version of an omelet, served open face. The frittata is cooked on one side, then flipped over so both the top and bottom are golden brown, allowing the eggs to set slowly.

Fusilli: A spiral pasta from southern Italy, usually served with spicy tomato sauces.

Gelato: Italian ice cream, usually prepared from an egg-based custard using whole milk or cream.

Genoa Salami: A fine-grind salami, moderately spiced, generally made from pork but sometimes beef or veal. Originally from Genoa, the popularity of this sausage has spread far beyond its birthplace.

Gnocchi: Any of several soft dumplings made from boiled potatoes, eggs and flour. They range from marble to golf-ball size and are boiled and served with a butter- or cream-based sauce.

Gnocchetti: A small, hard pasta dumpling that resembles a curly half-shell, served with tomato sauce.

Gorgonzola: A crumbly, cultured cheese similar to American blue cheese but with a sharper flavor. It originally came from the town of Gorgonzola, near Milan, in northern Italy.

Grappa: A brandy made from either grapes or apples. It is popular in northern Italian regions.

Linguine: A flat, thin noodle served with light sauces such as clam or pesto.

Marinara: A basic tomato sauce cooked by sautéeing onions and garlic in olive oil, then adding tomato pulp and spices.

Marsala: A dessert wine similar to sherry that can be sweet or dry. It is also used in meat dishes with veal or chicken.

Mascarpone: A smooth, mild soft cheese from northern Italy used as a spread or for making cheese-based desserts.

Minestra: A light soup with a broth base and pasta or vegetables. Not as thick as *zuppa*.

Monk Fish: A deep-water fish with a firm flesh and a mild, delicate flavor.

Morel Mushrooms: Spongelike small mushrooms with a meaty texture and nutty taste. They are eaten fresh, when available, or after they have been dried.

Mozzarella (Fresh): A Neapolitan cheese used in pizza, pastas and appetizers. Usually served in its original golf ball–size shape. When fresh it should be refrigerated and served within five days.

Mullet: A red-orange fish with a firm, white and flavorful meat.

Olives (Imported): Olives pickled in brine that are imported from Italy (Gaeta olives) or from Greece (Kalamata olives).

Olive Oil: (1) *All-purpose pure oil.* The juice of many different types of olives (including their kernels) extracted by heat processing. (2) *Virgin oil.* The juice extracted from the pulp of ripe olives. (3) *Extra-virgin oil.* This oil has the lowest acidity of all olive oils and is the juice extracted from ripe green olives by cold pressing them with stone grinders. This prevents any chemical alteration of the oil. It is the most flavorful oil and, along with other grades of olive oil, plays a fundamental part in the Mediterranean diet.

Pancetta: Italian bacon that is salted rather than smoked. It is generally rolled up, not flat like American bacon.

Parmesan: A hard cheese excellent for grating made from cow's milk; it originated in the city of Parma. Authentic cheese has the "Parmigiano Reggiano" seal all around its hard rind and has a flaky, dry consistency when cut. Romano cheese has similar characteristics, but it is saltier and made from sheep's milk.

Pear-shaped Tomatoes or Plum Tomatoes: Originally developed and grown in San Marzano, near Naples. These are the most suitable tomatoes for sauces, having the lowest acidity, most pulp and fewest seeds of all tomatoes.

Penne: A short-cut pasta about 1¼ inches long. Tubular in shape with slanted cuts at both ends, penne can be *lisce* (smooth) or *rigate* (with a grooved finish). Excellent with tomato and vegetable sauces.

Pesto: A sauce found throughout Italy in several versions, but always with the same base—basil, garlic and olive oil. Originally from Genoa, it was a "paste" made by pounding basil, garlic and pine nuts in a mortar with a pestle and then lacing with Parmesan or Romano cheese, pepper and olive oil. It is excellent served as a sauce for pasta or added to soups.

Piccata: Term indicating a "piquant" spicy sauce used to cook chicken or veal, in which the pungent flavors of capers, lemon juice and wine are combined.

Pignoli: Italian name for pine nuts, extracted from large pinecones. They are used to make sauces, desserts, eggplant salads and other dishes.

Polenta: A staple of northern Italy, polenta is made from cornmeal and traditionally eaten in place of bread or pasta. After cooking it can be served cold or baked with tomato sauce and cheese.

Pollo: The Italian word for a young chicken.

Porcini Mushrooms: Delicious, reddish brown-capped mushrooms with a yellow-orange meaty pulp. Sometimes called steak mushrooms after the flavor they develop when grilled.

Primavera: Translation of "springtime." Generally this term indicates a sauce for pasta prepared with fresh vegetables such as broccoli, cauliflower, peas and mushrooms.

Prosciutto: A lean, salt-cured ham traditionally aged for one year and served in paper-thin slices. Used in several appetizers, it is excellent with ripe cantaloupe and frequently combined with veal. If aged correctly it should have a tender texture and minimal salt flavor.

Provolone: A cheese with a sharp flavor similar to but stronger than mozzarella cheese. This southern Italian cheese takes many forms and sometimes it has a stringlike texture. After it has aged, its flavor is more pungent and the cheese can be used for grating.

Radicchio: A small leaf lettuce grown in Treviso in northern Italy. It has a red-purple color with white streaks and a strong, slightly bitter flavor. Radicchio is valued for its digestive properties.

Ragù Bolognese: *See* Bolognese Sauce.

Ravioli: Pillow-shaped pasta popular in several Italian regions, usually made with a stuffing of spinach and cheese. Ravioli are also filled with less common ingredients such as crabmeat or pumpkin. Traditionally served with plain butter and Parmesan, this pasta also is also delicious with tomato and meat sauces.

Ricotta: Fresh, soft cheese, which is similar to cultured cottage cheese; it is excellent in salads and as a stuffing for pastas and desserts.

Rigatoni: Short-cut, wide tubular pasta with lengthwise grooves, about 1 inch long.

Risotto: The traditional rice dish of northern Italy, prepared by making a soffrito (see below) of vegetables such as onion, garlic and parsley with butter or oil, and then gradually adding liquid, usually broth, while the rice cooks at medium heat to a creamy consistency.

Rockfish: A saltwater fish with a flavor and shape similar to bass.

Romano: A dry, firm grating cheese made from sheep's milk.

Rosamarina: A tiny bead-shaped noodle, ideal for use in soups.

Rotini: A short-cut pasta with a corkscrew shape.

Saffron: A pungent spice that comes from the dried stigmata of crocuses. It is used in several Mediterranean countries and gives a red-yellow color to the food it spices.

Saltimbocca: Literally "jump in the mouth." This term generally refers to a folded-over slice of meat filled with cheese, herbs or other meats that is quickly fried in a pan and eaten while piping hot.

Sambuca: A liqueur with the sweet, persistent flavor of anise, usually served with espresso coffee beans floated on top. Generally served after dinner with dessert or espresso.

Savoiardi: Ladyfinger-shaped cookies that are used to dip into coffee or tea and also as a base for several Italian desserts.

Semolina: A coarse flour made from milling the whole kernel of durum wheat. This is the flour used for traditional pasta dough and is high in fiber and protein.

Soffritto: An Italian term similar to "sauté," it is a mixture that forms the base of many sauces. Onion, garlic and other vegetables and herbs are quickly fried in oil or butter. Soffritto is usually cooked until sizzling and gives important flavor to many dishes.

Stromboli: A type of stuffed pizza in which the melted cheese and sauce filling flows from the dough similar to the flow of lava from the top of the Stromboli volcano in southern Italy.

Sugo Sauce: A light, mild tomato sauce traditionally prepared with a soffritto of onion, garlic and basil to which crushed tomatoes are added.

Tortelli: Literally translated this means "little torte," it is a round type of ravioli.

Tortellini: Little rings of pasta filled with cheese, originally from the city of Bologna. Usually served with tomato sauce, tortellini is added to traditional soups throughout Italy.

Tripe: Translation of *trippa,* part of a cow's stomach, usually sold precooked. It is generally cut into strips, boiled and then baked with a tomato sauce and vegetables.

Veal Scaloppine: Thin cut of veal loin that is cooked quickly and usually served with a wine, mushroom or cream sauce.

Verde: This literally means "green," and is the term used for a sauce with lots of olive oil, parsley, green onions or other greens.

Vermicelli: A very thin pasta.

Ziti: A short-cut pasta with a tubular shape.

Zuppa: The Italian word for "soup," zuppa specifically refers to a very thick soup in which vegetables are the main ingredients.

CHAPTER ONE

Antipasti

*Mixed-Antipasto Platter
(page 5), Cheese Pillows
(page 8)
Above: Doorway in
Populonia, Tuscany*

ANTIPASTO

Antipasto *literally means "before the pasta" and is served as an appetizer. In Italy almost all antipasto dishes are prepared in advance and served at room temperature, though a few are served warm. Antipasto tempts the eater visually as well as with its taste, and a colorful antipasto reflects the creativity of the cook as well as stimulates the appetite.*

EGGPLANT APPETIZER

Caponata Semplice

6 SERVINGS

2 large eggplant
1 tablespoon salt
1 cup olive oil
18 imported Italian black olives, pitted
8 fresh pear-shaped tomatoes, chopped
2 cloves garlic, finely chopped
1 tablespoon large capers, drained
2 tablespoons red-wine vinegar
1 tablespoon pine nuts
2 teaspoons sugar
1 teaspoon pepper

◆ Pare eggplant; cut into ½-inch cubes. Spread eggplant on cutting board; sprinkle with salt. Tilt board slightly; let stand 30 minutes.

Heat oil in 10-inch skillet over medium-high heat. Sauté olives, tomatoes, garlic and capers in oil. Rinse eggplant; pat dry. Stir eggplant and remaining ingredients into olive mixture. Cook uncovered over medium heat 20 minutes, stirring frequently. Serve hot or cold.

FRESH-SAGE FRITTERS

Frittelle di Salvia

12 FRITTERS

Vegetable oil
24 fresh large sage leaves
2 jumbo eggs
1 tablespoon all-purpose flour
½ teaspoon salt
½ teaspoon pepper
12 flat fillets of anchovy in oil, drained

◆ Heat oil (1 inch) in deep fryer or Dutch oven to 375°. Wash sage leaves; pat dry. Mix eggs, flour, salt and pepper until well blended. Dip 2 sage leaves into egg mixture. Place 1 fillet of anchovy on 1 leaf; top with second leaf.

Fry about 30 seconds or until crisp; drain on paper towels. Repeat with remaining sage leaves and fillets of anchovy.

SAVORY TOMATO APPETIZER

Pomodori Saporiti

6 SERVINGS

18 pickled imported Italian black
  olives, pitted
6 large tomatoes, cubed
1 small red onion, thinly sliced
  and separated into rings
1 cup diced Genoa salami (about
  8 ounces)
½ cup chopped fresh basil
½ cup shredded mozzarella
  cheese (2 ounces)
¼ cup freshly grated Parmesan
  cheese
3 tablespoons olive oil
1 tablespoon large capers,
  drained
1 teaspoon salt
½ teaspoon pepper
1 teaspoon red-wine vinegar

◆ Mix all ingredients. Cover and refrigerate at least 2 hours but no longer than 4 hours.

DEVILED EGGS

Uova alla Diavola

6 SERVINGS

6 hard-cooked jumbo eggs
2 ounces prosciutto or fully
  cooked Virginia ham
1 can (2½ ounces) tuna in oil,
  drained
2 tablespoons mayonnaise or
  salad dressing
3 flat fillets of anchovy in oil
1 teaspoon dry mustard
½ teaspoon white pepper
1 green onion (with top), finely
  chopped, or 2 tablespoons
  chopped chives

◆ Cut peeled eggs lengthwise in half. Slip out yolks. Place yolks and remaining ingredients except onion in food processor or in blender; cover and process until smooth. Fill whites with egg-yolk mixture, mounding it lightly. Sprinkle with onion. Cover and refrigerate no longer than 24 hours.

TYPES OF ANTIPASTO

There are three basic types of antipasto. Freddi e crudi includes raw vegetables and cold meats, fish and cheese. These can be served by themselves, such as carpaccio, or in various combinations. Affettati includes cured meats that are sliced just before serving and are accompanied by crusty breads or breadsticks. Prosciutto is the most popular example, and is served by itself or with fresh cantaloupe or fresh figs. Antipasti caldi are fried or baked morsels, just large enough to take the edge off a diner's hunger without being filling. They range from batter fritters such as fried zucchini blossoms to baked mussels and seasoned bread tarts such as bruschette and crostini.

PARMESAN AND ROMANO CHEESE

Parmesan and Romano are two favorite Italian cheeses, used in many dishes. Parmesan comes from the district of Parma in northern Italy and is usually aged for more than a year before it is sold. It has a dense texture and flakes easily when grated for topping pasta. It holds its shape when used for baking, and is used for dishes such as Eggplant Parmigiana and Veal Parmigiana.

CHICKEN ANTIPASTO

Pollo in Insalata

6 SERVINGS

2 heads Boston lettuce
2 poached or grilled boneless chicken breasts (about 1 pound), cut into ½-inch strips
12 flat fillets of anchovy in oil
1 red bell pepper, cut into strips
2 tablespoons mayonnaise or salad dressing
2 tablespoons extra-virgin olive oil
1 tablespoon large capers, drained
1 teaspoon soy sauce
1 small red chili, seeded and finely chopped
12 imported Italian black olives, pitted and sliced
3 hard-cooked eggs, sliced
Italian parsley sprigs

◆ Wash lettuce and cut into ½-inch strips. Line serving platter with lettuce. Alternate layers of chicken, fillets of anchovy and bell pepper on lettuce. Mix mayonnaise, oil, capers, soy sauce and chili; spread over top of layered antipasto. Arrange olives and eggs around edge of platter. Cover and refrigerate 2 to 4 hours or until chilled. Garnish with parsley.

CAVIAR TARTS

Tartine al Caviale

6 SERVINGS

12 slices crusty Italian bread or Vienna bread, each ½ inch thick
2 cloves garlic
4 ounces Mascarpone or cream cheese, softened
1 small white onion, grated
2 tablespoons chopped fresh tarragon
1 jar (1 ounce) black caviar, drained
½ teaspoon white pepper

◆ Trim crusts from bread. Cut each slice bread into 2-inch triangles. Toast in 375° oven 8 minutes, turning once, until golden brown. Cut each clove garlic in half; rub cut sides over both sides of toast triangles. Beat cheese, onion and tarragon until smooth. Stir in caviar and white pepper. Spread mixture over half of the toast triangles; top with remaining toast triangles. Secure with wooden picks.

MIXED-ANTIPASTO PLATTER

Antipasto Composto

6 TO 8 SERVINGS

2 cloves garlic
24 slices hard-crusted Italian
    bread, each ½ inch thick
12 slices prosciutto or fully cooked
    Virginia ham, cut in half
12 slices Provolone cheese, cut
    in half
24 slices Genoa salami
24 marinated mushrooms
24 marinated artichoke hearts
24 pickled imported Italian black
    olives, pitted
½ cup extra-virgin olive oil
Juice of ½ lemon
½ teaspoon dried oregano

◆ Cut each clove garlic in half; rub cut sides over both sides of bread. Arrange bread in single layer on serving platter. Top each bread slice with prosciutto, cheese, salami, mushrooms, artichoke hearts and olives. Drizzle with oil. Squeeze lemon juice over top; sprinkle with oregano.

SPICY EGGPLANT

Melanzane Piccanti

9 SERVINGS

4 medium eggplant
1 teaspoon salt
⅓ cup olive oil
½ medium red onion, chopped
2 cloves garlic, finely chopped
3 tablespoons pine nuts
2 tablespoons large capers,
    drained
½ cup milk
⅓ cup red-wine vinegar
2 teaspoons grated lemon peel
¼ cup butter
2 tablespoons chopped fresh
    parsley
2 small red chilies, seeded and
    finely chopped
¼ cup freshly grated Romano
    cheese

◆ Pare eggplant; cut into ½-inch cubes. Spread eggplant on cutting board; sprinkle with salt. Tilt board slightly; let stand 30 minutes.

Heat oil in 1½-quart saucepan over medium-high heat. Sauté onion, garlic, pine nuts and capers in oil. Stir in milk, vinegar and lemon peel. Reduce heat to low. Cook uncovered 20 minutes, stirring frequently.

Rinse eggplant; pat dry. Heat butter in 12-inch skillet over low heat until melted. Add eggplant; cook uncovered 20 minutes, stirring occasionally. Stir in milk mixture, parsley and chilies. Cook uncovered 15 minutes, stirring occasionally. Sprinkle with cheese.

PARMESAN AND ROMANO CHEESE

Romano cheese is made from sheep's milk, not cow's milk as is Parmesan. There are two types of Romano cheese in Italy—Pecorino Romano, from Rome, and Pecorino Sardo, from the island of Sardinia. Romano has a drier, sharper flavor than Parmesan, and is well suited for pastas served with cured meats such as prosciutto or bacon. It can be added to salads for extra flavor, or eaten with bread and a glass of wine. Its more pungent flavor is due to the diet of the sheep, which graze in sparse pastures, unlike the cows, which graze in the fertile fields of northern Italy and produce Parmesan.

BAKED FENNEL

Finocchi al Forno

4 TO 6 SERVINGS

4 large bulbs fennel
4 cups water
1 teaspoon salt
1 large cucumber
½ cup olive oil
1 pound fresh pear-shaped to-
    matoes, chopped*
1 tablespoon chopped fresh basil
1 cup Italian-style dry bread
    crumbs
¼ cup diced prosciutto or fully
    cooked Virginia ham (about
    2 ounces)
1 cup shredded mozzarella
    cheese (4 ounces)
1 tablespoon large capers,
    drained
1 tablespoon butter, softened

◆ Cut stems and outer leaves from fennel bulbs. Cut fennel bulbs crosswise into thin slices. Wash fennel with cold water; drain. Heat water and salt to boiling; add fennel. Reduce heat to medium. Boil uncovered 7 minutes or until tender; drain.

Cut cucumber lengthwise into fourths; cut fourths crosswise into ½-inch slices. Heat oil over medium-high heat. Sauté cucumber, tomatoes and basil in oil.

Heat oven to 375°. Grease rectangular baking dish, 13 × 9 × 2 inches; sprinkle with ¼ cup of the bread crumbs. Layer half of each of the fennel, prosciutto, tomato mixture, cheese and remaining bread crumbs in dish; repeat. Sprinkle with capers; dot with butter. Bake uncovered 20 minutes or until hot and bread crumbs are golden brown.

*1 can (28 ounces) imported pear-shaped tomatoes, drained and chopped, can be substituted for the fresh tomatoes.

Italians harvest fennel in the winter, providing a welcome vegetable in those cold months. The tops are used in soups and stews, as well as for seasoning and garnish. The bulbs can be eaten raw or cooked as in this savory appetizer. Fennel's refreshing flavor is an excellent accompaniment for meat dishes or rich holiday meals. Its aromatic seeds are a staple seasoning for cured meats, and fennel seeds—with their pungent anise flavor—are available commercially, whole or ground.

BASIL TOAST

Crostini al Basilico

6 SERVINGS

1 cup chopped tomatoes
3 tablespoons chopped fresh
  basil
1 tablespoon large capers,
  drained
½ teaspoon salt
½ teaspoon pepper
12 slices crusty Italian bread,
  each ½ inch thick
¼ cup extra-virgin olive oil
12 slices mozzarella cheese

◆ Heat oven to 375°. Mix tomatoes, basil, capers, salt and pepper. Place bread slices on ungreased cookie sheets. Drizzle 1 teaspoon oil on each slice bread. Spoon half of the tomato mixture over bread slices; top each with cheese slice. Spoon remaining tomato mixture over cheese. Bake uncovered 8 minutes or until hot and cheese is melted.

The literal translation of this recipe title is Cheese on a Chariot because it's quick to prepare—and eaten just as quickly. From Naples, this is a delicious example of how simple ingredients can make a very special dish.

CHEESE PILLOWS

Mozzarella in Carrozza

6 SERVINGS

Vegetable oil
12 slices crusty Italian bread or
  Vienna bread, each ½ inch
  thick
6 slices mozzarella or Bel Paese
  cheese, each ½ inch thick
6 flat fillets of anchovy in oil
2 jumbo eggs
½ teaspoon salt
½ teaspoon white pepper
1 cup warm milk
½ cup all-purpose flour

◆ Heat oil (2 inches) in deep fryer or Dutch oven to 375°. Trim crusts from bread. Place 1 slice cheese and 1 fillet of anchovy on each of 6 slices bread. Top with remaining bread slices.

Beat eggs, salt and white pepper in pie plate. Drizzle milk over both sides of sandwiches. Coat with flour; dip into egg mixture. Fry about 40 seconds or until golden brown.

Basil Toast, Caviar Tarts (page 4)

SPICY MEATBALLS

Polpettine Piccanti

6 SERVINGS

1 pound extra-lean ground beef
1 teaspoon freshly grated
    Parmesan cheese
1 teaspoon dried oregano
½ teaspoon dried basil
½ teaspoon garlic salt
½ teaspoon pepper
1 jumbo egg
2 tablespoons lemon juice
¼ cup olive oil
1 clove garlic, finely chopped
1 small red chili, seeded and
    finely chopped
½ red onion, finely chopped
1½ pounds fresh pear-shaped to-
    matoes, chopped*
1 tablespoon Chianti or dry red
    wine

◆ Mix ground beef, cheese, oregano, basil, garlic salt, pepper, egg and lemon juice. Shape mixture into 1-inch balls.

Heat oil in 10-inch skillet over medium-high heat. Sauté garlic, chili and onion in oil. Add meatballs. Cook, turning meatballs, until meatballs are brown. Stir in tomatoes and wine; reduce heat. Cover and simmer 30 minutes, stirring occasionally. Serve in chafing dish if desired.

*1 can (28 ounces) imported pear-shaped tomatoes, drained and chopped, can be substituted for the fresh tomatoes.

SEASONED ESCARGOTS

Lumache Profumate

6 TO 8 SERVINGS

In Italy, it is common to buy snails from street vendors after heavy rains, or to gather one's own snails. Typically, captive snails are fed bread or lettuce for a few days, then prepared for cooking by soaking in water and vinegar. After boiling, snails are sautéed and sauced. They are a common—not just a gourmet—treat.

24 fresh or canned snails in
    shells
2 tablespoons olive oil
2 cloves garlic, finely chopped
1 medium stalk celery, finely
    chopped
1 teaspoon chopped fresh parsley
1 teaspoon chopped fresh sage
10 walnut halves
1 teaspoon chopped fresh dill
1 teaspoon chopped fresh thyme
½ teaspoon salt
½ teaspoon pepper
2 tablespoons butter, softened

◆ Rinse snails with hot water; drain. Heat oil in 8-inch skillet over medium-high heat. Sauté garlic, celery and parsley in oil. Stir in snails and sage. Cook uncovered 5 minutes, stirring occasionally.

Place walnuts, dill, thyme, salt and pepper in food processor or in blender. Cover and process until walnuts are finely chopped. Stir walnut mixture into butter.

Heat oven to 450°. Fill shells with snail mixture. Dot each with butter mixture. Place shells in escargot pans or ungreased square pan, 8 × 8 × 2 inches. Bake uncovered 5 minutes or until hot.

SHRIMP WITH PROSCIUTTO

Scampi al Prosciutto

6 SERVINGS

2 tablespoons butter
2 tablespoons olive oil
2 flat fillets of anchovy in oil,
   finely chopped
1 tablespoon chopped fresh
   parsley
2 cloves garlic, finely chopped
18 jumbo raw shrimp in shells
9 thin slices prosciutto or fully
   cooked Virginia ham, cut in
   half crosswise
½ cup dry white wine
1 to 2 tablespoons lemon juice

◆ Heat oven to 375°. Heat butter and oil in square baking dish, 9 × 9 × 2 inches, in oven until butter is melted. Mix fillets of anchovy, parsley and garlic; spread evenly over butter mixture in baking dish.

Peel shrimp, leaving tails intact. Make a shallow cut lengthwise down back of each shrimp; wash out vein. Wrap one half-slice prosciutto around each shrimp. Place shrimp on anchovy mixture in baking dish. Bake uncovered 10 minutes. Pour wine and lemon juice over shrimp. Bake 10 minutes longer or until shrimp are done.

GOLDEN FRIED SQUID

Calamari Fritti

6 SERVINGS

Vegetable oil
1 pound cleaned fresh squid-tail
   cones (calamari)
1 egg, slightly beaten
1 tablespoon lemon juice
½ cup all-purpose flour
1 cup Italian-style dry bread
   crumbs
Salt and pepper to taste
1 lemon, sliced

◆ Heat oil (2 inches) in deep fryer or Dutch oven to 375°. Wash squid; pat dry. Cut squid into ¼-inch slices. Mix egg and lemon juice in small bowl. Coat squid with flour; shake off excess flour. Dip squid into egg mixture; coat with bread crumbs. Fry about 1 minute or until golden brown; drain on paper towels. Sprinkle with salt and pepper. Garnish with lemon slices and, if desired, parsley sprigs.

STUFFED MUSSELS

Cozze Ripiene

6 SERVINGS

24 fresh large mussels (about 2
    pounds)

⅓ cup olive oil

2 tablespoons chopped fresh
    parsley

4 large cloves garlic, finely
    chopped

½ cup Asti Spumante or dry
    white wine

½ cup Italian-style dry bread
    crumbs

1 tablespoon freshly grated
    Parmesan cheese

1 teaspoon finely chopped im-
    ported Italian black olives

¼ teaspoon salt

¼ teaspoon pepper

◆ Heat oven to 375°. Scrub and wash mussels with cold water, discarding any broken-shell or open (dead) mussels; drain. Heat oil in 12-inch skillet over medium-high heat. Sauté parsley and garlic in oil; add mussels and wine. Heat to boiling; reduce heat. Cover and simmer 5 minutes or until shells open. (Discard any mussels if shells do not open.)

Mix remaining ingredients. Remove top shell from mussels and discard. Place mussels in half shells in ungreased rectangular baking dish, 13 × 9 × 2 inches. Sprinkle about 1 teaspoon breadcrumb mixture over each mussel. Bake uncovered 20 minutes or until golden brown.

Mussels are an Italian seaside favorite, and the steamed mussels in this dish are succulent, nestling in their wine sauce. To clean mussels, scrub them thoroughly under running water, then soak in salted water (1 tablespoon of salt to 1 gallon of water) for one hour prior to cooking, and discard any mussels with open or broken shells. Before boiling, remove the mussel "beard"—the anchor that holds the mussel shell to the rocks—by holding the mussel in one hand and pulling the beard firmly with the other. This will ensure that the mussel is tender when cooked.

Stuffed Mussels, Shrimp with Prosciutto (page 11)

CHAPTER TWO

Soups

Summer Cold Soup (page 25), Orange-Lemon Sherbet (page 215)
Above: Villa garden in Capri

BEEF BROTH

Brodo di Carne

6 SERVINGS BEEF AND VEGETABLES
AND 12 TO 14 CUPS BROTH

2 tablespoons olive oil
4 cloves garlic, finely chopped
1 medium carrot, thinly sliced
1 medium stalk celery, thinly sliced
1 leek, thinly sliced
4 beef shanks (about 2 pounds)
4 beef short ribs (about 1½ pounds)
4 quarts water
1 tablespoon salt
1 teaspoon pepper
2 bay leaves

◆ Heat oil in 6-quart Dutch oven over medium-high heat. Sauté garlic, carrot, celery and leek in oil 5 minutes. Add beef shanks and short ribs. Cook beef, turning several times, until beef is brown. Add remaining ingredients. Heat to boiling; reduce heat to medium. Cover and cook 2 hours, skimming foam and fat from surface frequently.

Strain broth through cheesecloth-lined sieve. Beef and vegetables can be served immediately. Drizzle each serving with olive oil and lemon juice if desired. Use broth as directed in recipes calling for Beef Broth. Or cover and refrigerate up to 24 hours, or freeze for future use.

CHICKEN BROTH

Brodo di Pollo

8 TO 10 SERVINGS SOUP OR 12 TO 14 CUPS BROTH

2 tablespoons butter
2 cloves garlic, finely chopped
1 leek, thinly sliced
1 medium stalk celery, thinly sliced
1 medium carrot, thinly sliced
4- to 5-pound stewing chicken (with neck and feet, if desired)
4 quarts water
1 tablespoon salt
1 teaspoon white pepper
2 whole cloves
2 bay leaves

◆ Heat butter in 6-quart Dutch oven over medium-high heat. Sauté garlic, leek, celery and carrot in butter. Add chicken. Cook chicken, turning several times, until brown. Add remaining ingredients. Heat to boiling; reduce heat. Cover and simmer 1 hour, skimming fat from surface frequently.

Remove chicken from broth. Cool chicken about 10 minutes or until cool enough to handle. Remove skin and bones from chicken. Return chicken to broth. Heat to boiling; reduce heat. Cover and simmer 1 hour. Remove bay leaves.

Serve immediately as soup. Or strain broth through cheesecloth-lined sieve. Use broth as directed in recipes calling for Chicken Broth and cooked chicken in other recipes. Or cover and refrigerate up to 24 hours, or freeze for future use.

EGG DROP SOUP

Stracciatella

6 SERVINGS

4 cups Chicken Broth (see above)
2 cups water
½ cup uncooked rosamarina
2 eggs
1 teaspoon freshly grated nutmeg
½ teaspoon white pepper
⅓ cup all-purpose flour
½ cup freshly grated Parmesan cheese
1 tablespoon chopped fresh parsley

◆ Heat Chicken Broth and water to boiling in 4-quart Dutch oven; stir in rosamarina. Reduce heat to medium; cook uncovered 10 minutes.

Beat eggs, nutmeg and white pepper. Gradually stir in flour, beating until mixture is smooth. Slowly pour egg mixture into broth mixture, stirring constantly with wire whisk, until mixture is very thick. Cook uncovered 5 minutes, stirring occasionally. Top each serving with cheese and parsley.

Egg Drop Soup isn't found only in Oriental cuisine The Italian version was originally served when people were ill, because it is so easy to digest. It is generally made with semolina flour or some type of small pasta, as in this version, and herbs. In Rome fresh marjoram is used, and lemon juice is combined with the egg-broth mixture.

HOMEMADE MINESTRONE

Minestrone Casereccio

8 SERVINGS

2 beef shanks (about 1 pound)
1 tablespoon olive oil
1 clove garlic, finely chopped
½ small onion, chopped
2 large romaine leaves, torn into
    bite-size pieces
2 large red cabbage leaves,
    coarsely chopped
1 medium baking potato,
    chopped
1 medium carrot, chopped
4 quarts water
½ cup dried split peas
1 tablespoon salt
½ teaspoon pepper
2 medium stalks celery, chopped
2 fresh pear-shaped tomatoes,
    chopped*
1 bay leaf
1 cup uncooked rotini

◆ Remove bones and fat from beef shanks; cut beef into 1-inch pieces. Heat oil in 6-quart Dutch oven over medium-high heat. Sauté beef, garlic and onion in oil until beef is light brown.

Stir in romaine, cabbage, potato and carrot. Cook uncovered 5 minutes, stirring frequently, until romaine is wilted.

Stir in remaining ingredients except rotini. Heat to boiling; reduce heat. Cover and simmer 40 minutes. Stir in rotini; cover and simmer 10 minutes or until rotini is tender. Remove bay leaf.

*2 canned imported pear-shaped tomatoes can be substituted for the fresh tomatoes.

*Homemade Minestrone,
Spicy Breadsticks (page
119)*

This hearty soup recalls the simplicity of old-fashioned country meals. All the ingredients in this soup were available in farm kitchens—the bacon hung from the rafters, there was an ever-ready bag of potatoes and, just outside the kitchen door, dandelion greens, parsley, carrots and tomatoes could be picked.

FARMER'S SOUP

Minestra Contadina

6 SERVINGS

3 cups coarsely chopped dandelion greens* (about 6 ounces)
Juice of ½ lemon
¼ cup chopped lean bacon
2 tablespoons butter
2 leeks, cut into pieces
1 large potato, cut into pieces
1 large carrot, cut into pieces
1 clove garlic, chopped
½ cup chopped fresh parsley
8 cups water
1½ cups Chicken Broth (page 17)
1 cup fresh or frozen green peas
1 tablespoon canned tomato sauce
1 teaspoon salt
½ teaspoon pepper
2 tablespoons lemon juice

◆ Cover dandelion greens with cold water and juice of ½ lemon. Let stand 30 minutes; drain.

Cook bacon in butter in 4-quart Dutch oven over medium-low heat 8 minutes, stirring occasionally. Stir in dandelion greens. Cover and cook 10 minutes.

Place leeks, potato, carrot, garlic and parsley in food processor or blender; cover and process until finely chopped. Stir vegetable mixture into dandelion greens. Cook uncovered 10 minutes, stirring frequently. Stir in remaining ingredients. Heat to boiling; reduce heat to medium. Cover and cook 45 minutes, stirring occasionally.

*3 cups coarsely chopped escarole or curly endive can be substituted for dandelion greens.

LETTUCE SOUP

Zuppa di Lattuga

4 SERVINGS

2 tablespoons butter

I medium onion, finely chopped

I tablespoon chopped fresh
parsley

6 large iceberg lettuce leaves,
torn into bite-size pieces

6 large Boston or Bibb lettuce
leaves, torn into bite-size
pieces

6 large romaine leaves, torn
into bite-size pieces

2 cups water

4 cups Chicken Broth (page 17)

I egg yolk, slightly beaten

Juice of I lemon

I cup uncooked small macaroni
shells

¼ cup freshly grated Parmesan
cheese

◆ Heat butter in 3-quart saucepan over medium-high heat. Sauté onion and parsley in butter. Add lettuce and romaine; cover and cook over medium heat until wilted.

Stir in water, broth, egg yolk and lemon juice. Heat to boiling. Stir in macaroni; reduce heat to medium. Cover and cook 20 minutes or until macaroni is tender. Top each serving with cheese.

This is an excellent quick soup for busy days—in roughly half an hour you have the satisfaction of homemade soup, without the long cooking time.

FRESH MINT SOUP

Zuppa alla Menta

6 SERVINGS

1 large onion, chopped
¼ cup olive oil
1 pound lean bacon
6 fresh pear-shaped tomatoes,
    chopped*
3 medium zucchini, chopped
1 large potato, shredded
1 cup Chicken Broth (page 17)
1 cup water
¾ cup chopped fresh mint
1 teaspoon salt
½ teaspoon pepper
¼ cup chopped fresh mint

◆ Cover and cook onion in oil in 3-quart sauce-pan over medium-low heat 10 minutes. Trim excess fat from bacon; chop bacon. Stir into onion mixture. Cook uncovered over medium heat, stirring occasionally, until bacon is crisp. Stir in tomatoes, zucchini and potato. Cover and cook over medium-low heat 10 minutes.

Stir in remaining ingredients except ¼ cup mint. Heat to boiling; reduce heat. Cover and simmer 1 hour, stirring occasionally. Top each serving with mint.

*6 canned imported pear-shaped tomatoes can be substituted for the fresh tomatoes.

ONION AND POTATO SOUP

Zuppa di Patate e Cipolle

4 SERVINGS

2 large white onions, thinly sliced
3 tablespoons butter
2 tablespoons chopped fresh
    parsley
2 cloves garlic, finely chopped
2 bay leaves
½ cup diced prosciutto or fully
    cooked Virginia ham (about
    4 ounces)
4 cups Chicken Broth (page 17)
3 cups water
1 teaspoon pepper
4 large potatoes, shredded
¼ cup freshly grated Romano
    cheese

◆ Cover and cook onions in butter in 4-quart Dutch oven over medium-low heat 10 minutes. Stir in parsley, garlic, bay leaves and prosciutto. Cook uncovered over high heat 5 minutes, stirring frequently.

Stir in remaining ingredients except cheese. Heat to boiling; reduce heat. Cover and simmer 30 minutes, stirring occasionally. Remove bay leaves. Top each serving with cheese.

Mint is one of the oldest herbs used for both cooking and medicinal purposes, and its fresh scent captivates anyone who brushes past a mint plant. The ancient Romans learned its therapeutic uses from the Egyptians and introduced mint to other Mediterranean countries. Since ancient times it has been a favorite addition to sauces, vegetables, stuffings and soups. This mint soup has a refreshing lightness that is a pleasant alternative to the stronger spices used in many soups.

Fresh Mint Soup, Chunky Tomato Soup (page 24)

CHUNKY TOMATO SOUP

Pappa al Pomodoro

8 *SERVINGS*

Piazza in San Gimignano

2 tablespoons olive oil

4 cloves garlic, chopped

2 medium stalks celery, coarsely chopped

2 medium carrots, coarsely chopped

2 cans (28 ounces each) imported pear-shaped tomatoes, undrained

4 cups water

2 cans (14½ ounces each) clear chicken broth*

1 teaspoon dried basil

½ teaspoon pepper

2 bay leaves

8 slices hard-crusted Italian bread, each 1 inch thick

◆ Heat oil in 4-quart Dutch oven over medium-high heat. Sauté garlic, celery and carrots in oil. Stir in tomatoes; break up tomatoes coarsely. Stir in water, broth, basil, pepper and bay leaves. Heat to boiling; reduce heat. Cover and simmer 1 hour, stirring occasionally. Remove bay leaves.

Heat oven to 425°. Place bread on ungreased cookie sheet. Toast bread, turning once, until deep golden brown, about 6 minutes. Place 1 slice toast in each of 8 bowls. Ladle soup over toast; serve immediately.

*3½ cups Chicken Broth (page 17) can be substituted for the canned chicken broth.

BASIL RICE SOUP

Minestra di Riso e Basilico

6 *SERVINGS*

2 cloves garlic, finely chopped

2 medium celery stalks, chopped

1 medium onion, chopped

1 medium carrot, chopped

¼ cup chopped fresh basil

¼ cup olive oil

¾ cup uncooked regular rice

4 fresh pear-shaped tomatoes, chopped*

4 cups Chicken Broth (page 17)

1 cup water

1 teaspoon salt

½ teaspoon pepper

¼ cup freshly grated Romano cheese

◆ Cover and cook garlic, celery, onion, carrot and basil in oil in 4-quart Dutch oven over medium-low heat 10 minutes. Stir in rice and tomatoes. Cook uncovered over medium heat 5 minutes, stirring occasionally. Add remaining ingredients except cheese. Heat to boiling; reduce heat. Cover and simmer 20 minutes or until rice is tender. Top each serving with cheese.

*4 canned imported pear-shaped tomatoes can be substituted for the fresh tomatoes.

SUMMER COLD SOUP

Zuppa Estiva Fredda

4 SERVINGS

2 tablespoons olive oil

4 fresh pear-shaped tomatoes, chopped*

2 cloves garlic, finely chopped

4 slices prosciutto or fully cooked Virginia ham, cut into ¼-inch stips

2 medium cucumbers, pared, cut into fourths and sliced

2 cups whipping (heavy) cream

1 cup Chicken Broth (page 17)

1 teaspoon pepper

½ teaspoon salt

½ cup sliced green olives

1 green onion (with top), chopped

4 ice cubes

◆ Heat oil in 4-quart Dutch oven over medium-high heat. Sauté tomatoes and garlic in oil. Stir in prosciutto and cucumbers. Stir in whipping cream, Chicken Broth, pepper and salt.

Heat to boiling; reduce heat. Cover and simmer 40 minutes, stirring occasionally. Cover and refrigerate until chilled but no longer than 48 hours.

Ladle soup into 4 chilled individual bowls. Top each with olives, onion and ice cube.

*4 canned imported pear-shaped tomatoes can be substituted for the fresh tomatoes.

Cold soups are traditionally associated with French cuisine, but they are also found in northern Italy. They are as refreshing as they are convenient, and can be prepared ahead and served later—a boon on a busy day.

DUMPLING SOUP

Minestra di Gnocchi

6 SERVINGS

2 tablespoons olive oil

2 cloves garlic, finely chopped

1 medium onion, thinly sliced

1 pound chicken livers, cut up

4 cups Chicken Broth (page 17)

2 cups water

½ cup dry white wine

½ cup chopped fresh parsley

½ teaspoon pepper

1 bay leaf

1 medium potato, boiled, peeled and mashed (about ⅔ cup)

1 cup all-purpose flour

1 jumbo egg

◆ Heat oil in 4-quart Dutch oven over medium-high heat. Sauté garlic and onion in oil. Stir in chicken livers; cook over medium heat about 5 minutes, stirring frequently, until livers are brown. Stir in Chicken Broth, water, wine, parsley, pepper and bay leaf. Heat to boiling; reduce heat. Simmer uncovered 40 minutes.

Mix potato, flour and egg. Shape mixture into 1-inch balls. (Coat hands with flour, if necessary, to prevent sticking.) Remove bay leaf from soup. Heat soup to boiling; add dumplings. When dumplings rise to the surface, boil 4 minutes longer.

OAT SOUP

Zuppa d'Avena

2 tablespoons olive oil

2 medium potatoes, diced

2 medium carrots, diced

2 medium zucchini, diced

2 cloves garlic, finely chopped

1 medium onion, chopped

½ cup diced prosciutto or fully
  cooked Virginia ham (about
  4 ounces)

½ cup diced lean bacon

4 cups Chicken Broth (page 17)

2 cups water

1 tablespoon chopped fresh
  parsley

1 tablespoon chopped fresh basil

1 cup uncooked regular oats

6 slices hard-crusted Italian
  bread, toasted

1½ cups shredded Fontina
  cheese (6 ounces)

◆ Heat oil in 4-quart Dutch oven over medium-high heat. Sauté potatoes, carrots, zucchini, garlic and onion in oil 5 minutes. Stir in prosciutto and bacon. Cook uncovered over medium heat 10 minutes, stirring frequently. Add Chicken Broth, water, parsley and basil. Heat to boiling. Stir in oats; reduce heat. Cover and simmer 1 hour.

Ladle soup into 6 ovenproof bowls. Place 1 slice toast on soup in each bowl; top with cheese. Place bowls in jelly roll pan or on cookie sheet. Set oven control to broil. Broil soup with tops about 5 inches from heat 1 to 2 minutes or until cheese is melted and golden brown.

TORTELLINI SOUP

Tortellini in Brodo

8 TO 10 SERVINGS

2 cloves garlic, finely chopped
2 medium stalks celery, chopped
1 small onion, chopped
1 medium carrot, chopped
3 tablespoons butter
8 cups Chicken Broth (page 17)
4 cups water
2 packages (10 ounces each)
  dried cheese-filled tortellini
2 tablespoons chopped fresh
  parsley
½ teaspoon pepper
1 teaspoon freshly grated
  nutmeg
Freshly grated Parmesan cheese

◆ Cover and cook garlic, celery, onion and carrot in butter in 6-quart Dutch oven over medium-low heat 10 minutes. Stir in Chicken Broth and water. Heat to boiling; reduce heat. Stir in tortellini; cover and simmer 20 minutes, stirring occasionally, or until tortellini are tender.

Stir in parsley, pepper and nutmeg. Cover and cook 10 minutes. Top each serving with cheese.

CLAM CHOWDER
Zuppa d'Arselle

4 TO 6 SERVINGS

1/4 cup olive oil

3 tablespoons chopped fresh parsley

4 cloves garlic, finely chopped

2 green onions (with tops), finely chopped

1 small red chili, seeded and finely chopped

1 pound shucked fresh clams, drained and chopped

1 can (28 ounces) imported pear-shaped tomatoes, drained

8 cups water

1/2 cup dry white wine

1 1/2 teaspoons salt

1/2 teaspoon pepper

1 cup uncooked ditalini

◆ Heat oil in 4-quart Dutch oven over medium-high heat. Sauté parsley, garlic, onions and chili in oil. Stir in clams; cover and cook 5 minutes.

Place tomatoes in food processor or blender; cover and process until finely chopped. Stir tomatoes, water, wine, salt and pepper into clams. Heat to boiling; reduce heat. Cover and simmer 40 minutes, stirring occasionally. Stir in ditalini. Cover and cook 10 minutes or until ditalini are tender.

LENTIL SOUP
Zuppa di Lenticchie

4 TO 6 SERVINGS

1 1/2 cups dried lentils (about 1/2 pound)

2 tablespoons olive oil

2 cloves garlic, finely chopped

1 medium onion, finely chopped

1 bay leaf

1/2 cup diced prosciutto or fully cooked Virginia ham (about 4 ounces)

1/4 cup diced Genoa salami (about 2 ounces)

3 cups water

2 cups Chicken Broth (page 17)

1 teaspoon salt

1/2 teaspoon pepper

◆ Wash and sort lentils. Heat oil in 4-quart Dutch oven over medium-high heat. Sauté garlic, onion and bay leaf in oil. Stir in prosciutto and salami. Cook uncovered over medium heat 10 minutes, stirring frequently. Stir in lentils and remaining ingredients. Heat to boiling; reduce heat. Cover and simmer 1 hour, stirring occasionally. Remove bay leaf.

PASTA AND BEAN SOUP

Pasta e Fasuli

6 TO 8 SERVINGS

½ cup dried lima beans

½ cup dried kidney beans

½ cup dried split peas

½ cup chopped lean bacon

2 cloves garlic, finely chopped

2 medium stalks celery, finely
    chopped

1 medium carrot, finely chopped

1 medium onion, finely chopped

2 tablespoons olive oil

4 cups Chicken Broth (page 17)

4 cups water

1 cup uncooked rigatoni

1 teaspoon salt

½ teaspoon pepper

2 bay leaves

◆ Cover beans and peas with cold water. Let stand at room temperature at least 12 hours; drain.

Cook bacon, garlic, celery, carrot and onion in oil in 6-quart Dutch oven over medium heat 10 minutes, stirring occasionally. Stir in bean mixture and remaining ingredients. Heat to boiling; reduce heat. Cover and simmer 50 minutes, stirring occasionally. Remove bay leaves.

Fresco detail from a church in the Trastevere section of Rome

CREAM OF SPINACH SOUP

Minestra di Spinaci

6 SERVINGS

2 tablespoons olive oil

2 tablespoons butter

2 tablespoons chopped fresh
    parsley

4 cloves garlic, finely chopped

1 leek, thinly sliced

1 pound fresh spinach, torn into
    bite-size pieces

2 cups whipping (heavy) cream

2 cups milk

2 cups Chicken Broth (page
    17)

1 tablespoon lemon juice

1 teaspoon freshly grated
    nutmeg

1 teaspoon salt

½ teaspoon white pepper

◆ Heat oil and butter in 4-quart Dutch oven over medium-high heat. Sauté parsley, garlic and leek in oil mixture. Add spinach; cook uncovered over low heat 10 minutes, stirring frequently. Stir in whipping cream, milk, Chicken Broth and lemon juice. Heat to boiling; reduce heat. Cover and simmer 1 hour, stirring occasionally. Stir in remaining ingredients.

CREAM OF BROCCOLI SOUP

Crema ai Broccoli

12 SERVINGS

1½ pounds broccoli

2 tablespoons butter

2 cloves garlic, finely chopped

1 small onion, finely chopped

3 cups whipping (heavy) cream

2 tablespoons lemon juice

2 medium stalks celery, chopped

2 bay leaves

1 can (14½ ounces) clear
   chicken broth*

3 cups milk

2 tablespoons chopped fresh
   parsley

1 teaspoon ground sage or
   freshly grated nutmeg

½ teaspoon pepper

2 tablespoons freshly grated
   Parmesan cheese

◆ Cut broccoli flowerets from stems; reserve. Chop broccoli stems. Heat butter in 4-quart Dutch oven over medium-high heat. Sauté garlic and onion in butter. Stir in broccoli stems, whipping cream, lemon juice, celery, bay leaves and broth. Heat to boiling. Boil uncovered 15 minutes; reduce heat to medium. Stir in broccoli flowerets, milk, parsley, sage and pepper. Cover and cook 30 minutes. Remove bay leaves. Top each serving with cheese.

*1¾ cups Chicken Broth (page 17) can be substituted for the canned chicken broth.

SPICY CREAM OF TOMATO SOUP

Crema Piccante al Pomodoro

4 SERVINGS

2 tablespoons butter

2 large potatoes, diced

1 medium stalk celery, thinly
   sliced

1 medium onion, thinly sliced

1 red chili, seeded and finely
   chopped

1½ cans (28 ounces each)
   imported pear-shaped tomatoes, drained and chopped

1 tablespoon all-purpose flour

4 cups Beef Broth (page 16)

1 cup whipping (heavy) cream

1 cup seasoned croutons

½ teaspoon white pepper

◆ Heat butter in 4-quart Dutch oven over medium-high heat. Sauté potatoes, celery, onion, chili and tomatoes in butter. Sprinkle flour over vegetables; stir well. Remove from heat. Stir Beef Broth and whipping cream into vegetables. Heat to boiling; reduce heat. Cover and simmer 40 minutes, stirring occasionally.

Carefully pour about half of the soup into food processor or blender; cover and process until smooth. Repeat with remaining soup. Top each serving with croutons and white pepper.

This soup is an excellent alternative to pasta as a first course—with its easy preparation and flavorful combination of tomatoes, cream and croutons.

Cream of Broccoli Soup

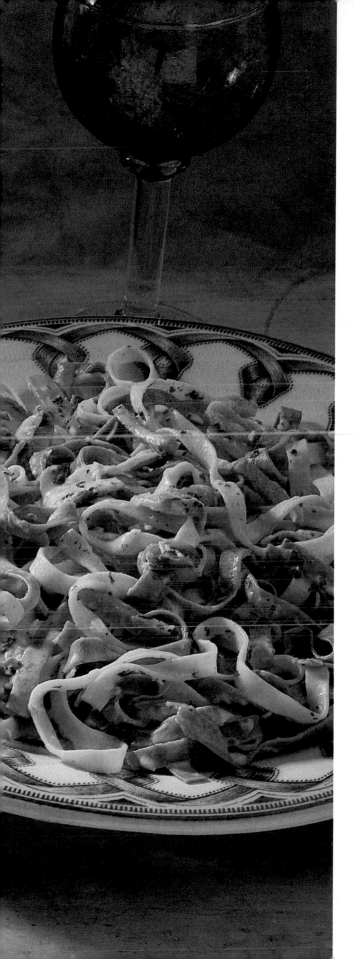

CHAPTER THREE

Pasta and Sauces

Straw and Hay Pasta
(page 47)
Above: Olive trees,
Populonia, Tuscany

EGG NOODLES

Pasta all'Uovo

24 OUNCES UNCOOKED NOODLES

3 cups semolina or all-purpose
  flour
4 jumbo eggs
¼ teaspoon salt
1 teaspoon olive oil

♦ Place flour in a mound on surface or in large bowl. Make a well in center of flour; add remaining ingredients. Mix thoroughly with fork, gradually bringing flour to center, until dough forms. (If dough is too sticky, gradually add flour when kneading. If dough is too dry, mix in enough water to make dough easy to handle.) Knead on lightly floured surface about 15 minutes or until smooth and elastic. Cover with plastic wrap or aluminum foil. Let stand 15 minutes.

Divide dough into 4 equal parts. (If desired, wrap unrolled dough securely and refrigerate up to 2 days. Let stand uncovered at room temperature 30 minutes before rolling and cutting.) Roll and cut as directed below.

MANUAL PASTA MACHINE: Flatten one part dough with hands to ½-inch thickness on lightly floured surface (keep remaining dough covered). Feed one part dough through smooth rollers set at widest setting. Sprinkle with all-purpose flour if dough becomes sticky. Fold lengthwise into thirds. Repeat feeding dough through rollers and folding into thirds 8 to 10 times or until firm and smooth. Feed dough through progressively narrower settings until dough is ⅛ to 1/16 inch thick. (Dough will lengthen as it becomes thinner; it may be cut crosswise at any time for easier handling.) Sprinkle dough lightly with all-purpose flour. Cut into ¼-inch strips for fettuccine, ⅛-inch strips for linguine.

HAND ROLLING: Roll each part dough with rolling pin into rectangle ⅛ to 1/16 inch thick on lightly floured surface. Sprinkle dough lightly with all-purpose flour. Loosely fold rectangle lengthwise into thirds; cut crosswise into ¼-inch strips for fettuccine, ⅛-inch strips for linguine. Shake out strips.

Arrange noodles in single layer on lightly floured towels; sprinkle lightly with all-purpose flour. (Or hang noodles on rack.) Let stand uncovered at room temperature 30 minutes.* Cook immediately as directed below, or cover and refrigerate up to 2 days, arranged in single layer on lightly floured towels.

Heat 4 quarts water and 1 tablespoon salt to boiling in large kettle; add noodles. Boil uncovered 2 to 4 minutes, stirring occasionally, until *al dente* (tender but firm). Begin testing for doneness when noodles rise to surface of water. Drain noodles. Do not rinse.

*If desired, let noodles stand at room temperature until completely dry. (Do not store until completely dry.) Dried noodles are very fragile; handle carefully. Cover loosely and store at room temperature up to 1 month.

HALF-RECIPE EGG NOODLES: Cut all ingredients in half. Continue as directed.

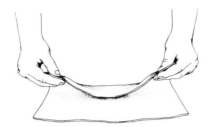

Fold one-third of dough lengthwise slightly over center.

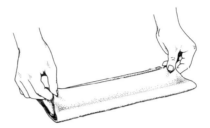

Bring remaining side over folded dough.

Cut crosswise into ¼-inch strips for fettuccine or ⅛-inch strips for linguine.

ALL-PURPOSE FLOUR

If semolina flour is not available, or if you are making pasta dough for the first time, all-purpose flour also produces excellent pasta. The dough will be less stiff and easier to handle. The amount of liquid you'll need will vary slightly, depending on the dryness of the flour as well as the temperature and humidity of your kitchen. If the dough is dry and crumbly, add water, a small amount at a time, until the dough is easy to handle but not too sticky.

COOKING PASTA

Pasta should be cooked al dente, or firm to the bite. Follow these tips for perfect al dente pasta.

1. Add salt to the water (1 tablespoon per gallon) to help keep noodles firm.

2. Use 1 gallon of water for each pound of pasta so pasta cooks uniformly.

3. Put oil in the water only if you plan to make a cold pasta salad, as it makes noodles slippery. Sauces cling much better to noodles boiled in salted water with no oil.

4. Water should always be at a full boil when pasta is added, and should remain at boiling during the entire cooking time.

5. When noodles are cooked, they will float to the top of the water. Test noodles on top of the water to check whether the pasta is done.

6. Never rinse pasta after draining, unless making a cold pasta dish. After draining, immediately mix warm pasta with sauce and serve at once.

SPINACH NOODLES

Pasta Verde

24 OUNCES UNCOOKED NOODLES

1 package (10 ounces) frozen chopped spinach
3 cups semolina or all-purpose flour
3 eggs
¼ teaspoon salt

◆ Cook spinach as directed on package; squeeze or press out liquid. Finely chop spinach, or place in food processor or in blender; cover and process until smooth.

Place flour in a mound on surface or in large bowl. Make a well in center of flour; add spinach, eggs and salt. Mix thoroughly with fork, gradually bringing flour to center, until dough forms. (If dough is too sticky, gradually add flour when kneading. If dough is too dry, mix in water.) Knead on lightly floured surface about 15 minutes or until smooth and elastic. Cover with plastic wrap or aluminum foil. Let stand 15 minutes.

Divide dough into 4 equal parts. (If desired, wrap unrolled dough securely and refrigerate up to 2 days. Let stand at room temperature 30 minutes before rolling and cutting.) Roll and cut as directed below.

MANUAL PASTA MACHINE: Flatten one part dough with hands to ½-inch thickness on lightly floured surface (keep remaining dough covered). Feed one part dough through smooth rollers set at widest setting. Sprinkle with all-purpose flour if dough becomes sticky. Fold lengthwise into thirds. Repeat feeding dough through rollers and folding into thirds 8 to 10 times or until firm and smooth. Feed dough through progressively narrower settings until dough is ⅛ to 1/16 inch thick. (Dough will lengthen as it becomes thinner; it may be cut crosswise at any time for easier handling.) Sprinkle dough lightly with all-purpose flour. Cut into ¼-inch strips for fettuccine, ⅛-inch strips for linguine.

HAND ROLLING: Roll each part dough with rolling pin into rectangle ⅛ to 1/16 inch thick on lightly floured surface. Sprinkle dough lightly with all-purpose flour. Loosely fold rectangle lengthwise into thirds; cut crosswise into ¼-inch strips for fettuccine, ⅛-inch strips for linguine. Shake out strips.

Arrange noodles in single layer on lightly floured towels; sprinkle lightly with all-purpose flour. (Or hang noodles on rack.) Let stand uncovered at room temperature 30 minutes.* Cook immediately as directed below, or cover and refrigerate up to 2 days, arranged in single layer on lightly floured towels.

Heat 4 quarts water and 1 tablespoon salt to boiling in large kettle; add noodles. Boil uncovered 2 to 4 minutes, stirring occasionally, until *al dente* (tender but firm). Begin testing for doneness when noodles rise to surface of water. Drain noodles. Do not rinse.

*If desired, let noodles stand at room temperature until completely dry. (Do not store until completely dry.) Dried noodles are very fragile; handle carefully. Cover loosely and store at room temperature up to 1 month.

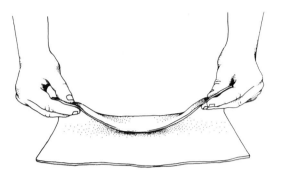

Fold one-third of dough lengthwise slightly over center.

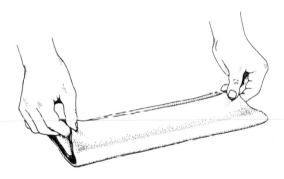

Bring remaining side over folded dough.

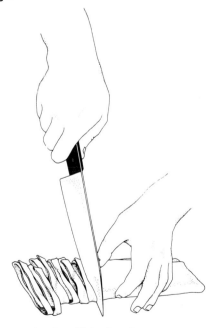

Cut crosswise into ¼-inch strips for fettuccine or ⅛-inch strips for linguine.

LINGUINE WITH FRESH BASIL-GARLIC SAUCE

Linguine al Pesto

4 SERVINGS

Egg Noodles (page 36)*
Basil-Garlic Sauce (page 85)
4 quarts water
1 tablespoon salt

◆ Prepare dough for Egg Noodles; roll and cut into linguine as directed. Remove one-third of the linguine and store for another use. Prepare Basil-Garlic Sauce.

Heat water and salt to boiling in large kettle; add linguine. Boil uncovered 2 to 4 minutes, stirring occasionally, until *al dente* (tender but firm). Begin testing for doneness when linguine rise to surface of water. Drain linguine. Do not rinse. Mix linguine and sauce.

*1 package (16 ounces) fresh or dried linguine can be substituted for the Egg Noodles. Cook as directed on package.

LINGUINE WITH SUGO SAUCE

Linguine al Sugo

4 SERVINGS

Egg Noodles (page 36)*
Sugo Sauce (page 84)
4 quarts water
1 tablespoon salt
2 tablespoons freshly grated
   Parmesan cheese

◆ Prepare dough for Egg Noodles; roll and cut into linguine as directed. Remove one-third of the linguine and store for another use. Prepare Sugo Sauce; keep warm.

Heat water and salt to boiling in large kettle; add linguine. Boil uncovered 2 to 4 minutes, stirring occasionally, until *al dente* (tender but firm). Begin testing for doneness when linguine rise to surface of water. Drain linguine. Do not rinse. Mix linguine and sauce; sprinkle with cheese.

*1 package (16 ounces) fresh or dried linguine can be substituted for the Egg Noodles. Cook as directed on package.

Linguine with Fresh Basil-Garlic Sauce

LINGUINE WITH CLAM SAUCE

Linguine alle Vongole

4 SERVINGS

DRAINING NOODLES

Draining noodles is an important step in preparing pasta dishes as it instantly stops the cooking. Draining should be done quickly, to prevent noodles from sticking together or cooling down. If the recipe calls for it, you can add some Parmesan cheese while mixing the noodles and sauce, to help sauce cling to the noodles. Don't add oil or rinse noodles in cold water (unless you are making a pasta salad), as it cools the noodles and makes them too slippery to receive a sauce.

Egg Noodles (page 36)*
Clam Sauce (page 84)
4 quarts water
1 tablespoon salt
Chopped fresh parsley

◆ Prepare dough for Egg Noodles; roll and cut into linguine as directed. Remove one-third of the linguine and store for another use. Prepare Clam Sauce; keep warm.

Heat water and salt to boiling in large kettle; add linguine. Boil uncovered 2 to 4 minutes, stirring occasionally, until *al dente* (tender but firm). Begin testing for doneness when linguine rise to surface of water. Drain linguine. Do not rinse. Mix linguine and sauce; sprinkle with parsley.

*1 package (16 ounces) fresh or dried linguine can be substituted for the Egg Noodles. Cook as directed on package.

Linguine with Clam Sauce

**Villa garden
in Capri**

LINGUINE WITH CHICKEN SAUCE

Linguine con Pollo

4 SERVINGS

Egg Noodles (page 36)*
2 tablespoons olive oil
2 medium green bell peppers,
    chopped
2 cloves garlic, finely chopped
1 medium onion, chopped (about
    ½ cup)
2 skinless, boneless chicken
    breast halves
4 cups chopped pear-shaped
    tomatoes**
1 tablespoon capers, drained
2 flat fillets of anchovy in oil,
    drained
1 cup sliced or chopped im-
    ported Italian black olives
1 teaspoon salt
½ teaspoon pepper
4 quarts water
1 tablespoon salt
2 tablespoons chopped fresh
    parsley
½ cup freshly grated Parmesan
    cheese

◆ Prepare dough for Egg Noodles; roll and cut into linguine as directed. Remove one-third of the linguine and store for another use.

Heat oil in 10-inch skillet over medium-high heat. Sauté bell peppers, garlic and onion in oil. Add chicken breast halves. Cook uncovered 5 minutes, turning once. Remove chicken; cut into ½-inch pieces. Stir chicken, tomatoes, capers, fillets of anchovy, olives, 1 teaspoon salt and the pepper into bell-pepper mixture. Cover and cook over medium-low heat 30 minutes, stirring occasionally.

Heat water and 1 tablespoon salt to boiling in large kettle; add linguine. Boil uncovered 2 to 4 minutes, stirring occasionally, until *al dente* (tender but firm). Begin testing for doneness when linguine rise to surface of water. Drain linguine. Do not rinse. Mix linguine and chicken mixture; top with parsley and cheese.

*1 package (16 ounces) fresh or dried linguine can be substituted for the Egg Noodles. Cook as directed on package.

**2 cans (28 ounces each) imported pear-shaped tomatoes, drained and chopped, can be substituted for the fresh tomatoes.

ANTONIO'S FETTUCCINE ALFREDO

Fettuccine Alfredo

4 SERVINGS

Egg Noodles (page 36)*
2 tablespoons butter
1 small onion, thinly sliced
4 cups whipping (heavy) cream
2 tablespoons freshly grated
   Parmesan cheese
1 teaspoon freshly grated
   nutmeg
1/2 teaspoon salt
1/2 teaspoon pepper
4 quarts water
1 tablespoon salt
2 tablespoons freshly grated
   Parmesan cheese
1 teaspoon freshly grated
   nutmeg
Freshly ground pepper

◆ Prepare dough for Egg Noodles; roll and cut into fettuccine as directed. Remove one-third of the fettuccine and store for another use.

Heat butter in 10-inch skillet over medium-high heat. Sauté onion in butter. Stir in whipping cream; heat to boiling. Stir in 2 tablespoons cheese, 1 teaspoon nutmeg, 1/2 teaspoon salt and 1/2 teaspoon pepper; reduce heat. Simmer uncovered 30 minutes, stirring frequently.

Heat water and 1 tablespoon salt to boiling in large kettle; add fettuccine. Boil uncovered 2 to 4 minutes, stirring occasionally, until *al dente* (tender but firm). Begin testing for doneness when fettuccine rise to surface of water. Drain fettuccine. Do not rinse. Mix fettuccine and sauce; top with 2 tablespoons cheese and 1 teaspoon nutmeg. Serve with pepper.

*1 package (16 ounces) fresh or dried fettuccine can be substituted for the Egg Noodles. Cook as directed on package.

Alfredo's was a popular restaurant in Rome, where the chef's fresh pasta was served at the table and topped with sauces made before the diner's eyes. Cream and Parmesan cheese form one of the most versatile sauces for pasta, and this sauce from Alfredo's served over fettuccine has become known as Fettuccine Alfredo. Antonio's variation of this classic is an adagio version, where the sauce is cooked at a slower pace, giving the cook time to prepare the noodles as the sauce simmers. The freshly grated nutmeg gives the dish a subtle flavor.

"BRAVO!" FETTUCCINE

Fettuccine alla "Bravo!"

6 SERVINGS

This sauce began as an experiment, combining the assertive flavor of the tomato-based Sugo Sauce that is a favorite of pasta lovers with the smoothness of cream. The addition of prosciutto and mushrooms makes this pasta a very satisfying meal.

4 cups Sugo Sauce (page 84)
Egg Noodles (page 36)*
2 tablespoons butter
1 cup sliced fresh mushrooms
½ cup chopped prosciutto or fully cooked Virginia ham (about 3 ounces)
2 green onions (with tops), thinly sliced
1 cup whipping (heavy) cream
½ teaspoon freshly grated nutmeg
½ teaspoon pepper
4 quarts water
1 tablespoon salt
½ cup freshly grated Parmesan cheese

◆ Prepare Sugo Sauce. Prepare dough for Egg Noodles; roll and cut into fettuccine as directed. Remove one-third of the fettuccine and store for another use.

Heat butter in 4-quart Dutch oven over medium-high heat. Sauté mushrooms, prosciutto and onions in butter. Stir in whipping cream, nutmeg and pepper. Heat to boiling; reduce heat. Simmer uncovered about 20 minutes, stirring frequently, until thickened. Stir in Sugo Sauce. Heat to boiling; reduce heat. Simmer uncovered 10 minutes, stirring occasionally.

Heat water and salt to boiling in large kettle; add fettuccine. Boil uncovered 2 to 4 minutes, stirring occasionally, until *al dente* (tender but firm). Begin testing for doneness when fettuccine rise to surface of water. Drain fettuccine. Do not rinse. Mix fettuccine and sauce; top with cheese.

*1 package (16 ounces) fresh or dried fettuccine can be substituted for the Egg Noodles. Cook as directed on package.

STRAW AND HAY PASTA

Paglia e Fieno

4 SERVINGS

Egg Noodles (page 36)*
Spinach Noodles (page 38)**
2 tablespoons butter
2 tablespoons chopped fresh
  parsley
1/2 small onion, chopped (about
  2 tablespoons)
1 1/2 cups sliced fresh mushrooms (about 4 ounces)
4 ounces fully cooked smoked
  ham, cut into 1 × 1/4-inch
  strips
1/4 cup brandy
1 cup whipping (heavy) cream
1/4 teaspoon salt
1/4 teaspoon pepper
4 quarts water
1 tablespoon salt
1 cup freshly grated Parmesan
  cheese
Freshly ground pepper

♦ Prepare dough for Egg Noodles and Spinach Noodles; roll and cut each into fettuccine as directed. Remove two-thirds of each fettuccine and store for another use.

Heat butter in 10-inch skillet over medium-high heat. Sauté parsley and onion in butter. Stir in mushrooms and ham. Cook about 5 minutes, stirring occasionally, until mushrooms are tender. Stir in brandy. Cook uncovered until liquid is evaporated. Stir in whipping cream, 1/4 teaspoon salt and 1/4 teaspoon pepper. Heat to boiling; reduce heat. Simmer uncovered about 15 minutes, stirring frequently, until thickened.

Heat water and 1 tablespoon salt to boiling in large kettle; add fettuccine. Boil uncovered 2 to 4 minutes, stirring occasionally, until *al dente* (tender but firm). Begin testing for doneness when fettuccine rise to surface of water. Drain fettuccine. Do not rinse. Mix fettuccine and sauce; top with cheese. Serve with pepper.

*8 ounces fresh or dried fettuccine can be substituted for the Egg Noodles. Cook as directed on package.

**8 ounces fresh or dried spinach fettuccine can be substituted for the Spinach Noodles. Cook as directed on package.

The "straw" in this delightful dish is the egg noodles; the "hay," the green spinach noodles. Its birthplace is Bologna, in northern Italy, which is known throughout the country as a bastion of glorious foods. When topped with a creamy mushroom sauce laced with brandy, it's hard to believe that the dish is so simple to prepare.

PASTA WITH COCOA AND CINNAMON
Pasta al Cacao e Cannella

4 SERVINGS

3 cups all-purpose flour

1 1/2 teaspoons cocoa

4 jumbo eggs

1/4 cup butter

2 teaspoons olive oil

1 green onion (with top), thinly sliced

4 quarts water

1 tablespoon salt

1/2 teaspoon ground cinnamon

◆ Place flour in a mound on surface or in large bowl. Make a well in center of flour; add cocoa and eggs. Mix thoroughly with fork, gradually bringing flour to center, until dough forms. (If dough is too sticky, gradually add flour when kneading. If dough is too dry, mix in water.) Knead on lightly floured surface about 10 minutes or until smooth. Cover with plastic wrap or aluminum foil. Let stand 15 minutes.

Divide dough into 4 equal parts. (If desired, wrap unrolled dough securely and refrigerate up to 2 days. Let stand at room temperature 30 minutes before rolling and cutting.) Roll and cut into fettuccine as directed in Egg Noodles (page 36). Cover noodles with plastic wrap until ready to use.

Heat butter and oil in 3-quart saucepan over medium heat. Sauté onion in butter mixture. Heat water and salt to boiling in large kettle; add noodles. Boil uncovered about 4 minutes, stirring occasionally, until *al dente* (tender but firm). Start testing for doneness when noodles rise to surface. Drain noodles; do not rinse. Add noodles to onion mixture. Sprinkle with cinnamon; toss.

In addition to the traditional white, yellow, green, red tomato and black squid-ink noodles, Florentine chefs made a red cocoa pasta, which was very popular in the nineteenth century. The Florentines, like many other cooks, used cocoa as a coloring and subtle flavoring, not just to flavor sweets. These noodles are not sweet, but they do have a lovely color.

Pasta with Cocoa and Cinnamon

**Statue in the Bomarzo
Gardens, near Rome**

BAKED LASAGNE
Lasagne al Forno

8 SERVINGS

*Half-Recipe Egg Noodles
  (page 37)**
2 tablespoons olive oil
4 cloves garlic, finely chopped
1 pound bulk Italian sausage
*1 medium onion, chopped (about
  ½ cup)*
*1 medium carrot, chopped
  (about ½ cup)*
*2 cans (28 ounces each) im-
  ported pear-shaped tomatoes, drained*
¼ cup packed fresh basil
½ teaspoon salt
½ teaspoon pepper
*4 cups shredded mozzarella
  cheese (16 ounces)*
*1 cup freshly grated Parmesan
  cheese*

◆ Prepare dough for Egg Noodles as directed; roll and cut into 6 rectangles, 12 × 4 inches. Cover rectangles with plastic wrap until ready to use. Heat oil in 10-inch skillet over medium-high heat. Cook garlic, sausage, onion and carrot in oil, stirring occasionally, until sausage is done; drain.

Place tomatoes and basil in food processor or in blender; cover and process until smooth. Stir tomato mixture, salt and pepper into sausage mixture. Heat to boiling; reduce heat. Simmer uncovered 30 minutes, stirring occasionally.

Heat oven to 375°. Grease rectangular baking dish, 13 × 9 × 2 inches. Mix cheeses. Place 2 rectangles in baking dish; top with half of the sausage mixture and one-third of the cheese. Repeat; top with remaining rectangles and cheese. Cover and bake about 40 minutes or until hot and bubbly. Let stand 15 minutes before cutting.

*12 dried lasagne noodles can be substituted for the Half-Recipe Egg Noodles. Cook noodles as directed on package. Assemble lasagne as directed above—except substitute 4 cooked dried lasagne noodles for the 2 fresh lasagne noodles.

SPINACH LASAGNE

Lasagne agli Spinaci

8 SERVINGS

Half-Recipe Egg Noodles (page 37)*

2 tablespoons butter

8 ounces fresh mushrooms, sliced

4 cloves garlic, finely chopped

1 medium onion, thinly sliced

1 medium carrot, thinly sliced

3 cups whipping (heavy) cream

2 tablespoons pine nuts

1 teaspoon freshly grated nutmeg

1 teaspoon salt

½ teaspoon pepper

4 cups shredded mozzarella cheese (16 ounces)

1 cup freshly grated Parmesan cheese

2 packages (10 ounces each) frozen chopped spinach, thawed and well drained

◆ Prepare dough for Egg Noodles as directed; roll and cut into 6 rectangles, 12 × 4 inches. Cover rectangles with plastic wrap until ready to use. Heat butter in 10-inch skillet over medium-high heat. Sauté mushrooms, garlic, onion and carrot in butter. Stir in whipping cream, pine nuts, nutmeg, salt and pepper. Heat to boiling; reduce heat. Simmer uncovered 30 minutes, stirring frequently, until thickened.

Heat oven to 375°. Grease rectangular baking dish, 13 × 9 × 2 inches. Mix cheeses. Place 2 rectangles in baking dish; top with half of the spinach and whipping-cream mixture and one-third of the cheese. Repeat; top with remaining rectangles and cheese. Cover and bake about 40 minutes or until hot and bubbly. Let stand 15 minutes before cutting.

*12 dried lasagne noodles can be substituted for the Half-Recipe Egg Noodles. Cook noodles as directed on package. Assemble lasagne as directed above—except substitute 4 cooked dried lasagne noodles for the 2 fresh lasagne noodles.

PASTA

Until the nineteenth century, Italian noodles were always manufactured during the summer and dried in the sun. When natural gas became available, hundreds of pasta factories throughout Italy began using gas-fired machines to dry dough, and pasta became available all year round. With the increased production, pasta was Inexpensively exported to other countries.

HALF-SHELL NOODLES WITH BROCCOLI AND RICOTTA SAUCE

Orecchiette alla Pugliese con Broccoletti   *6 SERVINGS*

Egg Noodles (page 36)
2 cloves garlic, finely chopped
2 tablespoons olive oil
*1 medium onion, chopped (about
  ½ cup)*
3 cups broccoli flowerets
1 cup whole milk
*½ cup Chicken Broth (page
  17)*
4 quarts water
1 tablespoon salt
16 ounces ricotta cheese
*½ cup freshly grated Parmesan
  cheese*
Freshly ground pepper

◆ Prepare dough for Egg Noodles as directed; do not roll or cut. Divide dough into 12 equal parts. Roll each part into a rope, ½ inch thick. Cut each rope into ½-inch pieces. Place cut sides down on lightly floured surface. Press thumb in center of each piece, forming half-shells. Place on lightly floured towels.

Heat oil in 10-inch skillet over medium-high heat. Sauté garlic and onion in oil. Stir in broccoli, milk and Chicken Broth. Heat to boiling; reduce heat. Cover and simmer about 10 minutes or until broccoli is tender.

Heat water and salt to boiling in large kettle; add noodles. Boil uncovered about 10 minutes, stirring occasionally, until *al dente* (tender but firm). Begin testing for doneness when noodles rise to surface of water. Drain noodles. Do not rinse. Mix broccoli mixture, ricotta and Parmesan cheeses; stir in noodles. Serve with pepper.

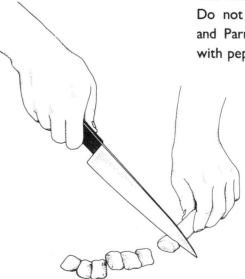

Cut each rope of dough into ½-inch pieces.

Place a piece of dough on surface, cut side down. Press thumb in center, rotating thumb slightly to form a round indentation.

CHEESE-FILLED NOODLES WITH FRESH MINT

Tortelli alla Menta

6 SERVINGS

Egg Noodles (page 36)
16 ounces ricotta cheese
½ cup chopped fresh mint
½ cup freshly grated Parmesan
  cheese
½ teaspoon freshly grated
  nutmeg
½ teaspoon salt
¼ cup butter
½ cup chopped fresh mint
¼ cup chopped fresh chives
½ cup whole milk
½ teaspoon freshly grated
  nutmeg
¼ teaspoon pepper
4 quarts water
1 tablespoon salt
½ cup freshly grated Parmesan
  cheese
Freshly ground pepper

◆ Prepare dough for Egg Noodles as directed; roll and cut into 14 rectangles, 12 × 4 inches. Cover rectangles with plastic wrap until ready to use.

Mix ricotta cheese, ½ cup mint, ½ cup Parmesan cheese, ½ teaspoon nutmeg and ½ teaspoon salt. Place ten 1-teaspoon mounds of cheese mixture about 1½ inches apart in 2 rows on one rectangle. Moisten dough lightly around mounds with water; top with second rectangle. Press gently around mounds to seal.

Cut around mounds using 2-inch tortelli cutter or round cookie cutter. Arrange in single layer on lightly floured towels; sprinkle lightly with all-purpose flour. Repeat with remaining cheese mixture and rectangles. Let stand uncovered at room temperature 30 minutes. Cook tortelli immediately as directed below, or cover and refrigerate up to 2 days arranged in single layer on lightly floured towels.

Heat butter in 2-quart saucepan over medium-high heat. Sauté ½ cup mint and the chives in butter. Stir in milk, ½ teaspoon nutmeg and ¼ teaspoon pepper. Heat to boiling, stirring frequently; reduce heat. Simmer uncovered 5 to 10 minutes or while cooking tortelli.

Heat water and 1 tablespoon salt to boiling in large kettle; add tortelli. Boil uncovered about 6 minutes, stirring occasionally, until *al dente* (tender but firm). Begin testing for doneness when tortelli rise to surface of water. Drain tortelli. Do not rinse. Mix tortelli, mint mixture and ½ cup Parmesan cheese. Serve with pepper.

t around mounds with 2-inch
nd cutter.

TORTELLI WITH CAVIAR SAUCE

Tortelli al Caviale

6 SERVINGS

Egg Noodles (page 36)
1 cup chopped fresh spinach
1 cup ricotta cheese, well
　drained
1 teaspoon freshly grated Ro-
　mano cheese
1 teaspoon freshly grated
　nutmeg
2 tablespoons butter
1 small onion, thinly sliced
1 red bell pepper, finely chopped
1/4 cup light rum
2 cups whipping (heavy) cream
1/4 teaspoon freshly grated
　nutmeg
1/4 teaspoon salt
1/4 teaspoon pepper
1 jar (4 ounces) black or red
　caviar, drained
4 quarts water
1 tablespoon salt
1/4 cup freshly grated Parmesan
　cheese

◆ Prepare dough for Egg Noodles as directed; roll and cut into 14 rectangles, 12 × 4 inches. Cover rectangles with plastic wrap until ready to use.

Mix spinach, ricotta and Romano cheeses and 1 teaspoon nutmeg. Place ten 1-teaspoon mounds of cheese mixture about 1½ inches apart in 2 rows on one rectangle. Moisten dough lightly around mounds with water; top with second rectangle. Press gently around mounds to seal.

Cut around mounds using 2-inch tortelli cutter or round cookie cutter. Arrange in single layer on lightly floured towels; sprinkle lightly with all-purpose flour. Repeat with remaining cheese mixture and rectangles. Let stand uncovered at room temperature 30 minutes. Cook tortelli immediately as directed below, or cover and refrigerate up to 2 days arranged in single layer on lightly floured towels.

Heat butter in 10-inch skillet over medium-high heat. Sauté onion and bell pepper in butter. Stir in rum; cook until liquid is evaporated. Stir in whipping cream, 1/4 teaspoon nutmeg, 1/4 teaspoon salt and the pepper. Heat to boiling; reduce heat. Simmer uncovered 30 minutes, stirring frequently. Stir in caviar. Cook 10 minutes longer, stirring frequently.

Heat water and 1 tablespoon salt to boiling in large kettle; add tortelli. Boil uncovered about 6 minutes, stirring occasionally, until *al dente* (tender but firm). Begin testing for doneness when tortelli rise to surface of water. Drain tortelli. Do not rinse. Pour sauce over tortelli; sprinkle with Parmesan cheese.

Tortelli with Caviar Sauce

SARDINIAN RAVIOLI WITH SUGO SAUCE

Ravioli Sardi al Sugo   *6 SERVINGS*

2 cups hot Sugo Sauce (page 84)

3 cups all-purpose flour

4 jumbo eggs

16 ounces fresh mozzarella or ricotta cheese

2 tablespoons chopped fresh parsley

2 tablespoons chopped fresh basil

1 tablespoon plus 1 teaspoon grated lemon peel

4 quarts water

1 tablespoon salt

◆ Prepare Sugo Sauce. Place flour in a mound on surface or in large bowl. Make a well in center of flour; add eggs. Mix thoroughly with fork, gradually bringing flour to center, until dough forms. (If dough is too sticky, gradually add flour when kneading. If dough is too dry, mix in water.) Knead on lightly floured surface about 10 minutes or until smooth and elastic. Cover with plastic wrap or aluminum foil. Let stand 15 minutes.

Divide dough into 4 equal parts. (If desired, wrap unrolled dough securely and refrigerate up to 2 days. Let stand at room temperature 30 minutes before rolling and cutting.) Roll as directed in Egg Noodles (page 36). Cut into 10 rectangles, 14 × 4 inches. Cover rectangles with plastic wrap until ready to use.

Press cheese through wire mesh of strainer. Mix cheese, parsley, basil and lemon peel. Place six 1-teaspoon mounds of cheese mixture about 1 inch apart in a single row lengthwise down center of one rectangle. Moisten dough lightly around mounds with water; fold rectangle lengthwise in half. Press gently around mounds to seal.

Cut around mounds into semicircle shapes; using 2-inch tortelli cutter or round cookie cutter. Arrange in single layer on lightly floured towels; sprinkle lightly with all-purpose flour. Repeat with remaining cheese mixture and rectangles. Let stand uncovered at room temperature 30 minutes. Cook ravioli immediately as directed below, or cover and refrigerate up to 2 days arranged in single layer on lightly floured towels.

Heat water and salt to boiling in large kettle; add ravioli. Boil uncovered about 6 minutes, stirring occasionally, until *al dente* (tender but firm). Begin testing for doneness when ravioli rise to surface of water. Drain ravioli. Do not rinse. Pour Sugo Sauce over ravioli.

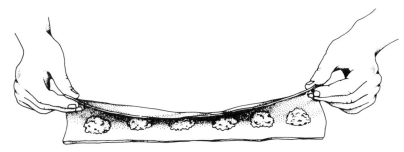

Place 6 mounds of cheese mixture down center of rectangle of dough. Fold rectangle lengthwise in half over cheese mixture.

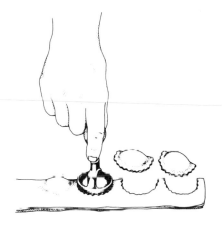

Cut into semicircle shapes along folded edge using 2-inch round cutter.

Following pages: Types of Pasta: (1) Vermicelli (2) Capellini (Angel Hair) (3) Rotini (4) Fusilli (5) Bucatini (6) Mafalde (7) Rigatoni (8) Lasagne (9) Orecchiette (10) Rosamarina (Orzo) (11) Farfalle (12) Gnocchi (13) Ziti (14) Baby Bow Ties (15) Penne (16) Ditalini (17) Medium Shells (18) Tortellini (19) Small Shells (20) Ravioli (21) Fettuccine

CHESTNUT-PUMPKIN RAVIOLI

Ravioli di Zucca e Castagne

6 SERVINGS

Pumpkin is a traditional pasta filling in northern Italy, and its delicate flavor is also used in desserts and with vegetables. Pumpkin seeds are a popular Italian snack, sold in street stands or at movie theaters— almost as popular as pop-corn is in America.

2 cups Sugo Sauce (page 84)
3 cups all-purpose flour
4 jumbo eggs
1 small pumpkin*
½ can (16-ounce size) chest-nuts, drained
½ cup freshly grated Parmesan cheese
1 teaspoon salt
1 teaspoon freshly grated nutmeg
½ teaspoon white pepper
2 tablespoons butter
1 pound bulk mild Italian sausage
1 medium onion, sliced
4 quarts water
1 tablespoon salt
Freshly grated Parmesan cheese

♦ Prepare Sugo Sauce. Place flour in a mound on surface or in large bowl. Make a well in center of flour; add eggs. Mix thoroughly with fork, gradually bringing flour to center, until dough forms. (If dough is too sticky, gradually add flour when kneading. If dough is too dry, mix in water.) Knead on lightly floured surface about 10 minutes or until smooth. Cover with plastic wrap or aluminum foil. Let stand 15 minutes. (Dough can be wrapped securely and refrigerated up to 2 days. Let stand at room temperature 30 minutes before rolling and cutting.)

Divide dough into 4 equal parts. Roll as directed in Egg Noodles (page 36). Cut into 10 rectangles, 14 × 4 inches. Cover rectangles with plastic wrap until ready to use.

Pare and seed pumpkin. Coarsely chop enough pumpkin to measure 1½ cups. Heat 1 inch water to boiling; add pumpkin and chestnuts. Cover and heat to boiling; reduce heat. Boil about 15 minutes or until pumpkin is tender; drain. Place pumpkin mixture in food processor or in blender; cover and process until smooth.

Mix pumpkin mixture, ½ cup cheese, 1 teaspoon salt, the nutmeg and white pepper. Place twelve 1-teaspoon mounds of pumpkin mixture about 1½ inches apart in 2 rows on one rectangle. Moisten dough lightly around mounds with water; top with second rectangle. Press gently around mounds to seal.

Cut between mounds into 12 squares using pastry cutter or knife. Arrange in single layer on lightly floured towels; sprinkle lightly with all-purpose flour. Repeat with remaining pumpkin mixture and rectangles. Let stand uncovered at room temperature 30 minutes. Cook ravioli immediately as directed below, or cover and refrigerate up to 2 days arranged in single layer on lightly floured towels.

Heat butter in 10-inch skillet over medium-high heat. Cook sausage and onion in butter, stirring occasionally, until sausage is brown. Stir in Sugo Sauce. Heat to boiling; reduce heat. Simmer uncovered 20 minutes.

Heat water and 1 tablespoon salt to boiling in large kettle; add ravioli. Boil uncovered about 6 minutes, stirring occasionally, until *al dente* (tender but firm). Start testing for doneness when ravioli rise to surface. Drain ravioli; do not rinse. Spoon sausage mixture over ravioli; sprinkle with cheese.

*1½ cups canned pumpkin can be substituted for the cooked fresh pumpkin. Cook chestnuts as directed—except omit adding pumpkin. Place canned pumpkin and cooked chestnuts in food processor or blender and continue as directed.

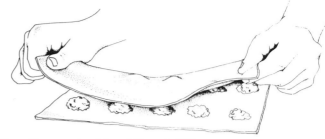

Place 12 mounds of pumpkin mixture about 1½ inches apart in 2 rows on one rectangle of dough. Top with second rectangle of dough.

Press gently around mounds to seal.

Cut between mounds using pastry cutter or knife.

RAVIOLI WITH BOLOGNESE SAUCE

Ravioli alla Bolognese

6 SERVINGS

Egg Noodles (page 36) or Spinach Noodles (page 38)
Bolognese Sauce (page 83)
1 cup chopped fresh spinach
16 ounces ricotta cheese
½ teaspoon freshly grated nutmeg
¼ teaspoon salt
4 quarts water
1 tablespoon salt
Freshly grated Parmesan cheese

♦ Prepare dough for Egg Noodles as directed; roll and cut into 14 rectangles, 12 × 4 inches. Cover rectangles with plastic wrap until ready to use. Prepare Bolognese Sauce; keep warm.

Mix spinach, ricotta cheese, nutmeg and ¼ teaspoon salt. Place ten 1-teaspoon mounds of cheese mixture about 1½ inches apart in 2 rows on one rectangle. Moisten dough lightly around mounds with water; top with second rectangle. Press gently around mounds to seal.

Cut between mounds into 10 squares using pastry cutter or knife.* Arrange in single layer on lightly floured towels; sprinkle lightly with all-purpose flour. Repeat with remaining cheese mixture and rectangles. Let stand uncovered at room temperature 30 minutes. Cook ravioli immediately as directed below, or cover and refrigerate up to 2 days arranged in single layer on lightly floured towels.

Heat water and 1 tablespoon salt to boiling in large kettle; add ravioli. Boil uncovered about 6 minutes, stirring occasionally, until *al dente* (tender but firm). Begin testing for doneness when ravioli rise to surface of water. Drain ravioli. Do not rinse. Top ravioli with sauce and sprinkle generously with Parmesan cheese.

*For round ravioli, cut with 2-inch tortelli cutter or round cookie cutter.

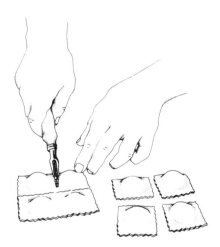

Cut between mounds using pastry cutter or knife.

TURKISH PASTA NESTS

Nidi di Pasta al Forno Turchi

5 SERVINGS

3 cups Sugo Sauce (page 84)
3 cups all-purpose flour
4 jumbo eggs
1/4 cup olive oil
1 leek, thinly sliced
1/2 pound ground lamb
1/4 cup chopped fresh mint
24 ounces ricotta cheese
1 cup finely chopped prosciutto
   or fully cooked Virginia
   ham (about 8 ounces)
1/2 cup freshly grated Parmesan
   cheese

◆ Prepare Sugo Sauce. Place flour in a mound on surface or in large bowl. Make a well in center of flour; add eggs. Mix thoroughly with fork, gradually bringing flour to center, until dough forms. (If dough is too sticky, gradually add flour when kneading. If dough is too dry, mix in water.) Knead on lightly floured surface about 10 minutes or until smooth. Cover with plastic wrap or aluminum foil. Let stand 15 minutes.

Divide dough into 5 equal parts. Roll each part as directed in Egg Noodles (page 36). Cut into 3 rectangles, 14 × 2 inches. Cover rectangles with plastic wrap until ready to use.

Heat oil in 10-inch skillet over medium-high heat. Cook leek and lamb in oil, stirring occasionally, until lamb is brown. Stir in Sugo Sauce and mint. Heat to boiling; reduce heat. Cover and simmer 20 minutes.

Heat oven to 350°. Spread 3 tablespoons each ricotta cheese and lamb mixture down center of each pasta rectangle. Roll up loosely, beginning at 2-inch side. Place rolls, spiral side up, in ungreased rectangular baking dish, 13 × 9 × 2 inches. Sprinkle prosciutto over rolls. Top with remaining ricotta cheese and lamb mixture and the Parmesan cheese. Bake uncovered 35 to 40 minutes or until hot.

When cheese melts over these little rolls of pasta, they resemble birds' nests, or Turkish turbans, which is how they received their name. The little rolls are easy to make using fresh pasta dough and there is no need to cook the pasta first as the dough is moist enough to roll easily. Be sure to use a pan no more than two inches deep or the rolls will not open slightly as they bake and form nests.

DANDELION-SPINACH PASTA ROLL

Rotolo di Spinaci e Denti di Leone   *4 SERVINGS*

Dandelions have long been enjoyed by the Italians. European settlers brought dandelions to America, where the blossoms were pickled like capers and the leaves cooked in soups or eaten in salads. Though not as widely eaten today, well-washed dandelions are a peppery addition to this dish. Dandelions should be picked when the buds are still closed, and if none are available, you can substitute escarole or curly endive.

1½ cups all-purpose flour
2 jumbo eggs
2 packages (10 ounces each) frozen chopped spinach
¼ pound fresh-picked dandelion greens, chopped*
16 ounces ricotta cheese
½ cup freshly grated Parmesan cheese
6 fresh sage leaves, chopped
½ teaspoon salt
½ teaspoon pepper
½ teaspoon freshly grated nutmeg
6 fresh sage leaves, chopped
½ cup butter

♦ Place flour in a mound on surface or in large bowl. Make a well in center of flour; add eggs. Mix thoroughly with fork, gradually bringing flour to center, until dough forms. (If dough is too sticky, gradually add flour when kneading. If dough is too dry, mix in water.) Knead on lightly floured surface about 10 minutes or until smooth. Cover with plastic wrap or aluminum foil. Let stand 15 minutes.

Cook spinach as directed on package—except add dandelion greens before cooking; drain. Cool 10 minutes. Mix spinach mixture, cheeses, 6 sage leaves, the salt, pepper and nutmeg.

Roll dough into rectangle, 14 × 12 inches, on lightly floured surface; spread with spinach mixture. Roll up, beginning at 14-inch side. Wrap roll in double layer of cheesecloth.

Heat 4 inches water to boiling in deep rectangular roasting pan. Place wrapped spinach roll in water (water should cover roll). Heat to boiling; reduce heat. Simmer uncovered 30 minutes. Carefully remove spinach roll; drain.

Cook 6 sage leaves in butter over low heat 5 minutes, stirring frequently. Unwrap spinach roll; cut into about 3-inch slices. Top with butter mixture.

*¼ pound escarole or curly endive can be substituted for dandelion greens.

Dandelion-Spinach Pasta Roll

NOODLES WITH SAFFRON SAUCE

Pasta allo Zafferano

6 SERVINGS

Saffron Noodles (below)
1/4 cup olive oil
2 cloves garlic, finely chopped
1 small red chili, seeded and
    finely chopped
8 ounces fresh mushrooms, sliced
1/2 pound ground pork
1 cup dry white wine
1 cup Chicken Broth (page 17)
1 package (.2 gram) saffron
    threads
4 quarts water
1 tablespoon salt
1/2 cup freshly grated Parmesan
    cheese
Freshly ground pepper

◆ Prepare Saffron Noodles. Heat oil in 10-inch skillet over medium-high heat. Sauté garlic and chili in oil. Stir in mushrooms and ground pork. Cook uncovered until pork is no longer pink. Stir in wine. Cook uncovered until liquid is evaporated. Stir in Chicken Broth and saffron. Heat to boiling; reduce heat. Simmer uncovered 15 minutes.

Heat water and salt to boiling in large kettle; add noodles. Boil uncovered 2 to 4 minutes, stirring occasionally, until *al dente* (tender but firm). Begin testing for doneness when noodles rise to surface of water. Drain noodles. Do not rinse. Pour sauce over noodles; sprinkle with cheese. Serve with pepper.

Saffron Noodles

4 cups semolina or all-purpose
    flour
5 jumbo eggs
1/2 teaspoon salt
1 package (.2 gram) saffron
    threads, crushed

Place flour in a mound on surface or in large bowl. Make a well in center of flour; add remaining ingredients. Mix thoroughly with fork, gradually bringing flour to center, until dough forms. (If dough is too sticky, gradually add flour when kneading. If dough is too dry, mix in water.) Knead on lightly floured surface about 15 minutes or until smooth and elastic. Cover with plastic wrap or aluminum foil. Let stand 15 minutes.

Divide dough into 4 equal parts. (If desired, wrap unrolled dough securely and refrigerate up to 2 days. Let stand at room temperature 30 minutes before rolling and cutting.) Roll and cut into fettuccine as directed in Egg Noodles (page 36).

Saffron is an exotic spice that adds a lovely yellow color as well as a special flavor to this dish. Saffron is an expensive item, but remember: A little bit goes a long way. There is a great deal of labor involved in harvesting saffron, which comes from extracting the orange pistils from the inner blossoms of a specific crocus—and there are only about four per plant. To make one pound of dry saffron, 70,000 flowers are harvested.

Arrange noodles in single layer on lightly floured towels; sprinkle lightly with all-purpose flour. (Or hang noodles on rack.) Let stand uncovered at room temperature 30 minutes.* Cook immediately as directed above, or cover and refrigerate up to 2 days, arranged in single layer on lightly floured towels.

*If desired, let noodles stand at room temperature until completely dry. (Do not store until completely dry.) Dried noodles are very fragile; handle carefully. Cover loosely and store at room temperature up to 1 month.

COAL MINER'S SPAGHETTI

Spaghetti alla Carbonara

6 SERVINGS

1 package (16 ounces) spaghetti
1 clove garlic, finely chopped
1 pound sliced lean bacon, cut into 1-inch pieces
1 tablespoon olive oil
3 eggs
1/4 cup freshly grated Parmesan cheese
1/4 cup freshly grated Romano cheese
2 tablespoons chopped fresh parsley
1/2 teaspoon pepper
Freshly grated Parmesan cheese
Freshly ground pepper

◆ Cook spaghetti as directed. Meanwhile cook and stir garlic and bacon in oil until bacon is crisp; drain. Mix eggs, 1/4 cup Parmesan cheese, the Romano cheese, parsley and 1/2 teaspoon pepper; reserve.

Drain spaghetti and immediately return to kettle over very low heat. Toss spaghetti quickly with egg mixture. Add bacon and olive oil mixture and stir. Top with Parmesan cheese; serve with pepper.

Coal miners are said to have invented this hearty and quick pasta dish, and American soldiers popularized it after Rome was liberated at the end of World War II.

SPAGHETTI IN PARCHMENT

Spaghetti al Cartoccio

4 SERVINGS

2 tablespoons olive oil
2 tablespoons chopped fresh
  parsley
2 cloves garlic, finely chopped
2 cups chopped cherry or pear-
  shaped tomatoes
1/2 cup dry white wine
1 package (8 ounces) spaghetti
1/4 cup freshly grated Parmesan
  cheese
2 tablespoons chopped fresh
  basil
1 tablespoon large capers,
  drained

◆ Heat oil in 10-inch skillet over medium-high heat. Sauté parsley and garlic in oil. Stir in tomatoes and wine. Heat to boiling; reduce heat. Cover and simmer 30 minutes, stirring occasionally.

Heat oven to 375°. Cook spaghetti as directed on package; drain. Mix spaghetti and sauce. Spread mixture lengthwise down center of double-thickness cooking parchment paper, 24 × 15 inches; sprinkle with cheese, basil and capers. Bring 24-inch sides of paper up over spaghetti; twist ends securely. Place on cookie sheet. Bake 8 minutes. To serve, carefully open center of parchment paper, leaving ends twisted.

Cooking food al cartoccio—in parchment paper—seals in the essence and moisture of the sauce. It gives the spaghetti in this recipe added flavor but allows it to remain moist and al dente (firm). It's also easy to serve: Carefully open the sealed top of the parchment paper and you have your own "serving bowl."

SPAGHETTI WITH MUSSEL SAUCE

Spaghetti al Sugo di Cozze

6 SERVINGS

2 pounds fresh mussels
2 tablespoons olive oil
2 tablespoons chopped fresh
  parsley
2 cloves garlic, finely chopped
2 cans (28 ounces each) imported pear-shaped tomatoes, drained and chopped
1 medium red bell pepper,
  chopped
1 package (16 ounces) spaghetti
1 tablespoon freshly grated
  Parmesan cheese
Freshly ground pepper

◆ Discard any broken-shell or open (dead) mussels. Wash remaining mussels, removing any barnacles with a dull paring knife. Remove beards by tugging them away from shells.

Heat oil in 10-inch skillet over medium-high heat. Sauté parsley and garlic in oil. Stir in tomatoes and bell pepper. Cook 5 minutes, stirring frequently, until pepper is tender.

Add mussels; cover and cook about 5 minutes or until mussels open. Discard unopened mussels. Remove mussels from shells and discard shells. Stir mussels into sauce.

Cook spaghetti as directed on package; drain. Mix spaghetti and sauce; top with cheese. Serve with pepper.

Spaghetti in Parchment

EGGPLANT AND SPAGHETTI ROLLS

Involtini di Maccheroni alle Melanzane   *6 SERVINGS*

When combined with pasta, eggplant doesn't need salting and draining time. A pleasant, meaty texture results from the combination of the eggplant and spaghetti, as their flavors blend together.

3 cups hot Sugo Sauce (page 84)
2 tablespoons olive oil
4 cloves garlic, finely chopped
I small red chili, seeded and finely chopped
2 cups fresh chopped pear-shaped tomatoes*
I package (8 ounces) spaghetti
2 large eggplant (about 1½ pounds each)
Vegetable oil
I cup ricotta cheese
½ cup freshly grated Parmesan cheese

♦ Prepare Sugo Sauce. Heat olive oil in 10-inch skillet over medium-high heat. Sauté garlic and chili in olive oil. Stir in tomatoes. Cover and cook over medium heat 45 minutes, stirring occasionally. Cook spaghetti as directed on package; drain. Toss with tomato mixture.

Pare eggplant; cut lengthwise into ¼- to ½-inch slices. Heat vegetable oil (about I inch) in 4-quart Dutch oven to 375°. Fry I or 2 eggplant slices at a time about I minute or until light brown; drain on paper towels.

Heat oven to 450°. Spread about ¼ cup spaghetti mixture on each eggplant slice. Roll up, beginning at narrow end. Place seam sides down in ungreased rectangular pan, 13 × 9 × 2 inches. Spread ricotta cheese over rolls; top with Sugo Sauce and Parmesan cheese. Bake uncovered about 25 minutes or until hot.

*I can (28 ounces) imported pear-shaped tomatoes, drained and chopped, can be substituted for the fresh tomatoes.

SPAGHETTI OF THE NIGHT

Spaghetti alla Puttanesca

4 SERVINGS

⅓ cup olive oil

2 cloves garlic, cut in half

1 tablespoon large capers, drained

4 flat fillets of anchovy in oil, drained

2 cans (28 ounces each) imported pear-shaped tomatoes, drained and chopped

1 small red chili, seeded and finely chopped

½ cup sliced imported Italian black olives

1 package (16 ounces) spaghetti

◆ Heat oil in 4-quart Dutch oven or 12-inch skillet over medium-high heat. Sauté garlic in oil until golden brown. Remove garlic and discard. Stir capers, fillets of anchovy, tomatoes and chili into oil in Dutch oven. Heat to boiling; reduce heat. Simmer uncovered 20 minutes. Stir in olives.

Cook spaghetti as directed on package; drain. Stir spaghetti into tomato mixture. Cook over high heat 3 minutes, stirring occasionally.

The ladies of the night in Naples are credited with making this dish popular. They liked it because it was fast and easy to cook, and it used a few inexpensive ingredients. It became popular with people from all walks of life, but kept the name "hooker's style" as a tribute to its origins. The captivating scent of this sauce still drifts through the narrow streets of Naples at dinnertime. And it's becoming popular in America as well, appearing on menus across the country under its Italian name, Spaghetti alla Puttanesca.

VERMICELLI WITH FRESH HERBS

Vermicelli alle Erbe Crude

6 SERVINGS

¼ cup olive oil

2 tablespoons chopped pine nuts

1 tablespoon chopped fresh parsley

1 tablespoon large capers, drained and chopped

2 teaspoons chopped fresh rosemary

2 teaspoons chopped fresh sage

1 teaspoon chopped fresh basil

1 pint cherry tomatoes, cut into fourths

1 package (16 ounces) vermicelli

Freshly ground pepper

◆ Mix oil, pine nuts, parsley, capers, rosemary, sage and basil. Stir in tomatoes. Cook vermicelli as directed on package; drain. Mix vermicelli and herb mixture. Serve with pepper.

Following pages: Vermicelli with Fresh Herbs, Angel Hair Pasta with Shrimp (page 75)

Hilltop villa in Tuscany

ZITI WITH ASPARAGUS SAUCE

Ziti agli Asparagi

6 SERVINGS

1½ pounds fresh asparagus
2 tablespoons butter
2 cloves garlic, finely chopped
1 leek, thinly sliced
1 cup Chicken Broth (page 17)
½ cup dry white wine
½ teaspoon pepper
1 package (16 ounces) ziti or
　other tubular pasta
¼ cup freshly grated Parmesan
　cheese

◆ Break off tough ends of asparagus where stalks snap easily. Cover asparagus with cold water. Let stand 1 hour.

Heat butter in 10-inch skillet over low heat. Stir in garlic and leek. Cover and cook 10 minutes. Stir in Chicken Broth, wine, pepper and asparagus. Heat to boiling; reduce heat. Cover and simmer about 10 minutes or until asparagus is tender.

Cut tips from 12 stalks of the asparagus; reserve. Place remaining asparagus mixture in food processor or in blender; cover and process until smooth.

Cook ziti as directed on package; drain. Mix ziti and sauce; top with asparagus tips and cheese.

ANGEL HAIR PASTA IN GARLIC SAUCE

Capelli d'Angelo Aglio e Olio

6 SERVINGS

1 package (16 ounces) capellini
　(angel hair pasta)
¼ cup olive oil
¼ cup chopped fresh parsley
4 cloves garlic, finely chopped
½ cup freshly grated Parmesan
　cheese
Freshly ground pepper

◆ Cook capellini as directed on package. Meanwhile, heat oil in 10-inch skillet over medium-high heat. Sauté parsley and garlic in oil. Drain capellini and mix with garlic mixture; top with cheese. Serve with pepper.

ANGEL HAIR PASTA WITH SHRIMP

Capellini ai Gamberetti

4 SERVINGS

*1 package (16 ounces) capellini
   (angel hair pasta)*
¼ cup olive oil
*2 tablespoons chopped fresh
   parsley*
2 cloves garlic, finely chopped
*1 small red chili, seeded and
   finely chopped*
⅓ cup dry white wine
*½ teaspoon freshly grated
   nutmeg*
*12 ounces frozen peeled raw
   small shrimp, thawed*

◆ Cook capellini as directed on package. Meanwhile, heat oil in 4-quart Dutch oven or 12-inch skillet over medium-high heat. Sauté parsley, garlic and chili in oil. Stir in wine, nutmeg and shrimp; reduce heat. Cover and simmer about 5 minutes or until shrimp are pink.

Drain capellini; mix with shrimp mixture in Dutch oven. Cook over medium heat 2 minutes, stirring occasionally.

LOVER'S-STYLE PASTA

Bucatini all'Amatriciana

4 SERVINGS

2 tablespoons olive oil
*1 tablespoon chopped fresh
   parsley*
1 teaspoon chopped fresh thyme
1 medium onion, thinly sliced
*1 small red chili, seeded and
   finely chopped*
*¼ pound sliced bacon, cut into
   1-inch pieces*
1 tablespoon balsamic vinegar
*4 cups fresh chopped pear-
   shaped tomatoes**
1 package (16 ounces) bucatini

◆ Heat oil in 4-quart Dutch oven or 12-inch skillet over medium-high heat. Sauté parsley, thyme, onion and chili in oil. Stir in bacon. Cook about 5 minutes, stirring frequently, until bacon is crisp; drain, reserving 2 tablespoons fat. Stir vinegar into Dutch oven; cook until evaporated. Stir in tomatoes and reserved bacon fat. Heat to boiling; reduce heat. Cover and simmer 20 minutes, stirring occasionally.

Cook bucatini as directed on package; drain. Mix bucatini and tomato mixture in Dutch oven. Cook over high heat 3 minutes, stirring constantly.

*2 cans (28 ounces each) imported pear-shaped tomatoes, drained and chopped, can be substituted for the fresh tomatoes.

Commonly called Lover's-style Pasta, this pasta actually originated in the town of Amatrice, near Rome, a heritage that is also reflected in its name. Every summer Amatrice holds a celebration where this luscious dish is cooked and served absolutely free to tourists, residents and other lovers of Bucatini all'Amatriciana.

SAVORY FUSILLI

Fusilli Saporiti

6 SERVINGS

¼ cup olive oil
1 tablespoon capers, drained
3 cloves garlic, finely chopped
2 cans (28 ounces each) imported pear-shaped tomatoes, drained and chopped
1 small red chili, seeded and chopped
½ cup sliced imported Italian black olives
½ cup sliced green olives
1 tablespoon chopped fresh oregano
1 tablespoon chopped fresh basil
1 package (16 ounces) fusilli (spiral pasta)
Freshly ground pepper

◆ Heat oil in 10-inch skillet over medium-high heat. Sauté capers and garlic in oil. Stir in tomatoes and chili. Heat to boiling; reduce heat. Cover and simmer 20 minutes, stirring occasionally. Stir in olives, oregano and basil. Cover and cook 10 minutes.

Cook fusilli as directed on package; drain. Mix fusilli and tomato mixture. Serve with pepper.

The enticing blend of seasonings in this sauce made it a favorite of the Savoy royal family, earning it the nickname "favorita"— favorite sauce.

BUTTERFLY PASTA WITH FAVORITE SAUCE
Farfalle alla Favorita

4 SERVINGS

2 tablespoons olive oil
2 cloves garlic, finely chopped
I small onion, chopped (about
   ¼ cup)
½ cup chopped prosciutto or
   fully cooked Virginia ham
   (about 3 ounces)
I small red bell pepper, finely
   chopped
I tablespoon dry white wine
I can (28 ounces) imported
   pear-shaped tomatoes,
   undrained
½ teaspoon pepper
I package (16 ounces) butterfly-
   shaped pasta
¼ cup freshly grated Parmesan
   cheese
I tablespoon chopped fresh
   basil

◆ Heat oil in 10-inch skillet over medium-high heat. Sauté garlic and onion in oil. Stir in prosciutto and bell pepper. Cook 5 minutes, stirring occasionally, until pepper is tender. Stir in wine. Cook uncovered until liquid is evaporated. Stir in tomatoes and pepper; break up tomatoes. Heat to boiling; reduce heat. Simmer uncovered 45 minutes, stirring occasionally.

Cook pasta as directed on package; drain. Mix pasta and sauce; top with cheese and basil.

SHELL MACARONI WITH LOBSTER

Gnocchetti all'Aragosta

6 SERVINGS

Sugo Sauce (page 84)
8 quarts water
2 tablespoons salt
2 tablespoons wine vinegar
2 live lobsters (about 1 pound each)
12 fresh sage leaves
1 package (32 ounces) large macaroni shells

◆ Prepare Sugo Sauce; keep warm. Heat water, salt and vinegar to boiling in large kettle. Plunge lobsters headfirst into water. Cover and heat to boiling; reduce heat. Simmer uncovered 10 to 12 minutes or until lobsters are bright red. Drain and cool slightly.

Place each lobster on its back; cut lengthwise in half. Remove the stomach, which is just behind the head, and the intestinal vein, which runs from the stomach to the tip of the tail. Do not discard the green liver and coral roe. Remove meat. Crack claws; remove meat. Stir lobster meat, liver, roe and sage leaves into Sugo Sauce. Heat to boiling; reduce heat. Simmer uncovered 10 minutes, stirring occasionally.

Cook macaroni as directed on package; drain. Pour sauce over macaroni.

Italians cook lobsters whole and use all of the meat, cracking shells lengthwise from tail to antennae. Nothing goes to waste, especially in sauces where the liver, eggs and stomach are used. This dish is best with fresh lobsters. Be sure to buy live lobsters with no cracks on their shells, and check to be sure the lobsters' claws are pegged and tied together. If live lobsters are unavailable, look for frozen lobster tails. Use two frozen tails to equal one whole lobster.

80

PENNE WITH RADICCHIO

Penne al Radicchio

6 SERVINGS

2 tablespoons olive oil
2 tablespoons butter
1 medium onion, thinly sliced
1 head radicchio, cut into ¼-inch
  strips
½ cup dry white wine
1 cup whipping (heavy) cream
½ teaspoon pepper
1 package (16 ounces) penne
½ cup freshly grated Parmesan
  cheese

◆ Heat oil and butter in 10-inch skillet over medium-high heat. Sauté onion in oil mixture. Stir in radicchio. Cover and cook over low heat 5 minutes or until tender. Stir in wine. Cook uncovered until liquid is evaporated. Stir in whipping cream and pepper. Heat to boiling; reduce heat. Simmer uncovered 30 minutes, stirring frequently, until thickened.

Cook penne as directed on package; drain. Mix penne and radicchio mixture; top with cheese.

PENNE WITH VODKA SAUCE

Penne alla Vodka

6 SERVINGS

This is a modern pasta recipe popular in northern Italy. Cooks were intrigued by different ways of cooking short-cut pastas, and found vodka to be an innovative addition to their repertoire. Brandy or grappa is sometimes substituted for the vodka.

3 tablespoons butter
1 tablespoon olive oil
2 cloves garlic, finely chopped
1 small onion, chopped (about
  ¼ cup)
¼ cup chopped prosciutto or
  fully cooked Virginia ham
2 skinless, boneless chicken
  breast halves, cut into
  ½-inch pieces
½ cup vodka
½ cup whipping (heavy) cream
½ cup sliced imported Italian
  black olives
1 tablespoon chopped fresh
  parsley
½ teaspoon pepper
1 package (16 ounces) penne
  or mostaccioli
2 tablespoons freshly grated
  Parmesan cheese

◆ Heat butter and oil in 10-inch skillet over medium-high heat. Sauté garlic and onion in butter mixture. Stir in prosciutto and chicken. Cook, stirring occasionally, until chicken is brown. Stir in vodka. Heat over high heat until hot.

Carefully ignite. Stir in whipping cream, olives, parsley and pepper when flame dies out.* Heat to boiling; reduce heat. Simmer uncovered 30 minutes, stirring frequently, until thickened.

Cook penne as directed on package. Mix penne and cream mixture; top with cheese.

*To extinguish flame easily, cover with lid.

Penne with Radicchio

ROTINI WITH FRESH HERBS

Rotini alle Erbette

6 SERVINGS

Hadrian's villa, near Tivoli

2 tablespoons chopped fresh
　mint
2 tablespoons chopped fresh
　parsley
2 tablespoons chopped fresh
　basil
2 tablespoons chopped fresh
　dill weed
1 pound fresh spinach*
1/2 cup water
2 tablespoons butter
2 cloves garlic, finely chopped
1 cup whipping (heavy) cream
1/2 teaspoon salt
1/2 teaspoon pepper
1 package (16 ounces)
　vegetable-flavored rotini
1/2 cup freshly grated Parmesan
　cheese

♦ Mix mint, parsley, basil and dill weed; cover with cold water. Let stand 1 hour; drain and pat dry.

Heat spinach and water to boiling. Cover and cook about 5 minutes or until tender; drain well. Heat butter in 10-inch skillet over medium-high heat. Sauté garlic in butter. Stir in herbs, spinach, whipping cream, salt and pepper. Heat to boiling; reduce heat. Cover and simmer 20 minutes, stirring frequently.

Cook rotini as directed on package; drain. Mix rotini and sauce; top with cheese. Garnish with fresh herb leaves if desired.

*1 package (10 ounces) frozen chopped spinach can be substituted for the fresh spinach. Cook as directed on package; drain well.

TORTELLINI WITH MUSHROOM AND BRANDY SAUCE

Tortellini alla Panna e Funghi

4 SERVINGS

Mushroom and Brandy Sauce
　(page 85)
1 package (16 ounces) fresh or
　dried cheese tortellini
1/2 cup freshly grated Parmesan
　cheese

♦ Prepare Mushroom and Brandy Sauce; keep warm. Cook tortellini as directed on package; drain. Mix tortellini and sauce; top with cheese. Serve with freshly ground pepper if desired.

SIMPLE PIZZA SAUCE

Salsa Semplice per Pizze

ABOUT 3 CUPS SAUCE

2 cans (28 ounces each) imported pear-shaped tomatoes, drained
1 tablespoon chopped fresh basil
1 ½ teaspoons dried oregano
1 teaspoon freshly grated Romano cheese
2 teaspoons extra-virgin olive oil
¼ teaspoon salt
¼ teaspoon pepper
4 cloves garlic

◆ Place all ingredients in food processor or blender; cover and process until smooth. Use immediately or cover and refrigerate sauce up to 48 hours. Freeze up to 2 months. Thaw in refrigerator before using.

BOLOGNESE SAUCE

Ragù Bolognese

ABOUT 6 CUPS SAUCE

2 tablespoons olive oil
2 tablespoons butter
2 medium carrots, chopped (about 1 cup)
1 medium onion, chopped (about ½ cup)
½ pound bulk Italian sausage
½ pound lean ground beef
½ cup dry red wine
3 cans (28 ounces each) imported pear-shaped tomatoes, drained and chopped
1 teaspoon salt
1 teaspoon dried oregano
½ teaspoon pepper

◆ Heat oil and butter in 4-quart Dutch oven over medium-high heat. Sauté carrots and onion in oil mixture. Stir in sausage and ground beef. Cook over medium heat, stirring occasionally, until done; drain. Stir in wine. Heat to boiling; reduce heat. Simmer uncovered until wine is evaporated. Stir in remaining ingredients. Heat to boiling; reduce heat. Cover and simmer 45 minutes, stirring occasionally.

Bologna is a noted food capital and is famous for its fresh filled tortellini and huge mortadella hams—the granddaddy of the meat we call Bologna ham. This is also the home of the classic Bolognese sauce, which has often been copied in America. This recipe is the authentic version of Bolognese sauce and may surprise you with its rich and subtle flavors.

CLAM SAUCE
Vongole

ABOUT 2½ CUPS SAUCE

¼ cup olive oil
3 cloves garlic, finely chopped
1 can (28 ounces) imported
  pear-shaped tomatoes,
  drained and chopped
1 small red chili, seeded and
  finely chopped
1 pint shucked fresh small
  clams, drained and chopped
  (reserve liquid)
1 tablespoon chopped fresh
  parsley
1 teaspoon salt

◆ Heat oil in 10-inch skillet over medium-high heat. Sauté garlic in oil. Stir in tomatoes and chili. Sauté 3 minutes. Stir in clam liquid. Heat to boiling; reduce heat. Simmer uncovered 10 minutes. Stir in clams, parsley and salt. Cover and simmer 30 minutes, stirring occasionally, until clams are tender.

Tomatoes were introduced to Europe after they were discovered in America, but they were used only as ornamental plants. Neapolitans were the first to use tomatoes as a food source, during a famine in the seventeenth century. The region around Naples is where the best pear-shaped tomatoes are grown and canned. They make excellent sauces, having more pulp, more sweetness and lower acidity than other tomatoes. The only substitute for imported Italian pear-shaped tomatoes in a sauce is fresh, vine-ripened tomatoes.

SUGO SAUCE
Sugo

ABOUT 4½ CUPS SAUCE

1 tablespoon olive oil
4 cloves garlic, finely chopped
1 small onion, chopped (about
  ¼ cup)
2 cans (28 ounces each) imported pear-shaped tomatoes, drained
2 tablespoons chopped fresh
  basil
2 tablespoons chopped fresh
  oregano
½ teaspoon salt
½ teaspoon pepper

◆ Heat oil in 3-quart saucepan over medium-high heat. Sauté garlic and onion in oil. Place tomatoes in food processor or in blender; cover and process until smooth. Stir tomatoes and remaining ingredients into mixture in saucepan. Heat to boiling; reduce heat. Simmer uncovered 45 minutes, stirring occasionally.

BASIL-GARLIC SAUCE

Pesto

ABOUT 1½ CUPS SAUCE

1 cup chopped fresh basil
½ cup freshly grated Parmesan
  cheese
½ cup pine nuts
½ cup chopped fresh parsley
½ cup olive oil
1 teaspoon salt
½ teaspoon pepper
8 cloves garlic

♦ Place all ingredients in food processor or in blender; cover and process until smooth.

MUSHROOM AND BRANDY SAUCE

Panna e Funghi

ABOUT 4½ CUPS SAUCE

2 tablespoons butter
2 cloves garlic, finely chopped
1 small onion, finely chopped
  (about ¼ cup)
8 ounces fresh mushrooms, thinly
  sliced
½ cup brandy
4 cups whipping (heavy)
  cream
½ teaspoon freshly grated
  nutmeg
½ teaspoon pepper

♦ Heat butter in 10-inch skillet over medium-high heat. Sauté garlic and onion in butter. Stir in mushrooms. Sauté 5 minutes. Stir in brandy. Heat to boiling. Carefully ignite. Stir in whipping cream, nutmeg and pepper when flame dies out.* Heat to boiling; reduce heat. Simmer uncovered 20 minutes, stirring frequently, until thickened.

*To extinguish flame easily, cover with lid.

Originally from Genoa, pesto is now used throughout Italy and America. It's a highly versatile sauce made with basil that adds fresh, pungent flavor to pasta, vegetables, bruschetta (toasted bread) and salads. There are variations on pesto using combinations of other herbs, including parsley and mint, and other nuts (such as walnuts) in the place of pine nuts, but the classic recipe here is favored over all. When you find fresh basil, be sure to make extra batches of pesto. You can freeze it for later use (don't add the cheese until you thaw the pesto), so you can enjoy a taste of summer all year long.

CHAPTER FOUR

Other First Courses

Risotto with Shrimp
(page 88)
Above: Trees line the road
in Baratti, Tuscany

RISOTTO

Northern Italians favor rice and cornmeal over pasta, using many variations of them. The classic rice dish is risotto, in which Arborio rice is cooked with broth and an almost endless variety of ingredients—such as meats and vegetables— to create a rice that is tender and creamy, yet which retains some firmness. The trick is in the slow cooking of the rice, judicious stirring and regulating the amount of liquid added. It's easy to learn to prepare a classic risotto such as Risotto with Gorgonzola Cheese (page 89) or a more unusual Strawberry Risotto (page 207).

RISOTTO WITH SHRIMP

Risotto ai Gamberi

6 SERVINGS

1 pound medium raw shrimp in shells
2 tablespoons butter
1 medium onion, thinly sliced
½ cup dry white wine
1½ cups uncooked Arborio rice
2 cups Chicken Broth (page 17)
1 cup water
¼ cup freshly grated Parmesan cheese
Freshly ground pepper

◆ Peel shrimp. Make a shallow cut lengthwise down back of each shrimp; wash out vein. Heat butter in 12-inch skillet or Dutch oven over medium-high heat. Sauté onion in butter. Reduce heat to medium; add shrimp. Cook uncovered about 8 minutes, turning once, until shrimp are pink. Remove shrimp from skillet; keep warm.

Add wine to mixture in skillet; cook until liquid is evaporated. Stir in rice. Cook uncovered over medium heat, stirring frequently, until rice begins to brown. Mix Chicken Broth and water; pour ½ cup mixture over rice. Cook uncovered, stirring occasionally, until liquid is absorbed. Repeat with remaining broth mixture, ½ cup at a time. Stir in shrimp. Sprinkle with cheese and pepper.

JULIENNE-STYLE RISOTTO

Risotto alla Giulia

6 SERVINGS

2 tablespoons olive oil
1 tablespoon butter
1 medium onion, thinly sliced
2 medium zucchini, cut into julienne strips
2 medium yellow bell peppers, cut into julienne strips
⅓ cup dry white wine
2 cups uncooked Arborio rice
3⅓ cups Chicken Broth (page 17)
1 cup whipping (heavy) cream
½ teaspoon pepper
2 tablespoons freshly grated Parmesan cheese

◆ Heat oil and butter in 12-inch skillet or Dutch oven over medium-high heat. Sauté onion in oil mixture. Stir in zucchini and bell peppers. Cook about 5 minutes, stirring frequently, until tender. Stir in wine; cook until liquid is evaporated. Reduce heat to medium; stir in rice. Cook uncovered, stirring frequently, until rice begins to brown.

Mix Chicken Broth, whipping cream and pepper; pour ½ cup mixture over rice. Cook uncovered, stirring occasionally, until liquid is absorbed. Repeat with remaining broth mixture, ½ cup at a time. Top with cheese.

RISOTTO WITH GORGONZOLA CHEESE

Risotto al Gorgonzola

6 SERVINGS

2 tablespoons butter
1 medium onion, thinly sliced
1 medium carrot, thinly sliced
2 cups uncooked Arborio rice
3⅓ cups milk
1⅓ cups whipping (heavy) cream
⅓ cup crumbled Gorgonzola or blue cheese
⅓ cup Bel Paese or cream cheese (about 3 ounces)
½ teaspoon pepper

◆ Heat butter in 12-inch skillet or Dutch oven over medium-high heat. Sauté onion and carrot in butter. Reduce heat to medium; stir in rice. Cook uncovered, stirring frequently, until rice begins to brown.

Mix milk and whipping cream; pour ½ cup mixture over rice. Cook uncovered, stirring occasionally, until liquid is absorbed. Repeat with remaining milk mixture, ½ cup at a time. Stir in cheeses and pepper. Cook about 5 minutes, stirring frequently, until cheeses are melted.

CHILLED RISOTTO SALAD

Risotto Freddo Estivo

6 SERVINGS

2 tablespoons butter
1 small onion, thinly sliced
1 medium carrot, thinly sliced
1 medium stalk celery, thinly sliced
2 cups uncooked Arborio rice
1 medium green bell pepper, chopped
3⅔ cups Chicken Broth (page 17)
1 cup water
1 can (6½ ounces) tuna in oil, undrained
1 tablespoon chopped fresh mint
1 cup mayonnaise or salad dressing
½ teaspoon white pepper
Parsley sprigs

◆ Heat butter in 12-inch skillet or Dutch oven over medium-high heat. Sauté onion, carrot and celery in butter. Reduce heat to medium; stir in rice and bell pepper. Cook uncovered, stirring frequently, until rice begins to brown.

Mix Chicken Broth and water; pour ½ cup mixture over rice. Cook uncovered, stirring occasionally, until liquid is absorbed. Repeat with remaining broth mixture, ½ cup at a time. Mix rice, tuna and mint; spoon into shallow serving dish. Cover and refrigerate about 2 hours or until chilled.

Mix mayonnaise and white pepper; spread over rice mixture. Garnish with parsley.

Rice salads have long been an elegant dish in northern Italy, especially in the regions surrounding Venice. Traditionally the rice is boiled in water or broth, then chilled. This dish gives creative cooks the opportunity to garnish the dish attractively with vegetables or to serve after molding into different shapes.

POLENTA WITH SAUSAGE

Polenta con Salsiccia

8 SERVINGS

Sugo Sauce (page 84)
4 cups water
1½ teaspoons salt
1½ cups yellow cornmeal
1 small onion, thinly sliced
1 pound bulk Italian sausage
1 tablespoon olive oil
½ cup freshly grated Parmesan
    cheese

◆ Prepare Sugo Sauce. Heat water and salt to boiling in Dutch oven. Gradually add cornmeal, stirring constantly. Reduce heat to low. Cook uncovered about 30 minutes, stirring frequently, until mixture is very thick and leaves side of Dutch oven. Spread polenta in ungreased square baking dish, 9 × 9 × 2 inches. Cover and keep warm.

Cook onion and sausage in oil in 10-inch skillet or Dutch oven, stirring frequently, until sausage is no longer pink. Stir in Sugo Sauce. Heat to boiling; reduce heat. Simmer uncovered 20 minutes, stirring occasionally. Cut polenta into pieces. Spoon sausage mixture over polenta; sprinkle with cheese.

POLENTA TIMBALE

Sformato di Polenta

16 SERVINGS

8 cups water
1 tablespoon salt
3 cups yellow cornmeal
1 cup sliced mushrooms
1 cup milk
½ cup chopped prosciutto or
    fully cooked Virginia ham
½ teaspoon freshly grated
    nutmeg

◆ Heat water and salt to boiling in Dutch oven. Gradually add cornmeal, stirring constantly. Reduce heat to low. Cook uncovered about 30 minutes, stirring frequently, until mixture is very thick and leaves side of Dutch oven. Stir in remaining ingredients. Cook 5 minutes, stirring frequently.

Spread in ungreased 12-cup bundt cake pan. Refrigerate at least 45 minutes. Invert onto serving plate; cut into slices.

POLENTA

Since its introduction to Italy, corn has been a staple in the regions surrounding Venice (Veneto, Lombardy, Piedmont, Emilia and Romagna). Italians have eaten polenta, made from cornmeal, for centuries; it is a favorite substitute for bread or pasta, served hot or cold. When warm, polenta is served with butter or cheese, or such meats as sausage, small game birds and even shellfish. Cold, polenta is just as versatile; it can be baked, fried, grilled or broiled. Try cutting cold polenta into cubes, covering them with tomato sauce and Parmesan cheese, and baking in a 375° oven for 20 minutes. Delicious!

Polenta with Sausage

It's simple to make classic grooved gnocchi by using a wooden or plastic butter paddle, available in gourmet or kitchen equipment stores. After forming gnocchi, roll them firmly over the grooved edges of the paddle to form grooves.

SPINACH GNOCCHI WITH NUTMEG

Gnocchi di Spinaci alla Noce Moscata

4 SERVINGS

1 medium baking potato (about 6 ounces)

½ teaspoon salt

1 teaspoon freshly grated nutmeg

1 jumbo egg

1 package (10 ounces) frozen chopped spinach, thawed and well drained

1 to 1⅓ cups all-purpose flour

2 tablespoons butter

2 green onions (with tops), thinly sliced

1 cup whipping (heavy) cream

¼ teaspoon white pepper

4 quarts water

1 tablespoon salt

¼ cup freshly grated Parmesan cheese

◆ Heat potato and enough water to cover to boiling. Cover and boil about 30 minutes or until tender; drain and cool slightly. Pare and mash potato; cool. Stir in ½ teaspoon salt, the nutmeg, egg, spinach and enough flour to make stiff dough. Shape into 1-inch balls.

Heat butter in 10-inch skillet over medium-high heat. Sauté onions in butter. Stir in whipping cream and white pepper. Heat to boiling; reduce heat. Simmer uncovered 10 minutes or until thickened.

Heat water and 1 tablespoon salt to boiling; add half of the gnocchi. After gnocchi rise to surface, boil 4 minutes. Remove with slotted spoon; drain. Repeat with remaining gnocchi. Mix gnocchi and cream mixture. Sprinkle with cheese.

Spinach Gnocchi with Nutmeg

POTATO GNOCCHI WITH PARSLEY SAUCE

Gnocchi in Salsa Verde

6 SERVINGS

2 medium baking potatoes
  (about 6 ounces each)
1 teaspoon salt
2 jumbo eggs
2 to 2⅓ cups all-purpose flour
1½ cups chopped fresh parsley
½ cup freshly grated Parmesan
  cheese
½ cup extra-virgin olive oil
2 tablespoons capers, drained
½ teaspoon pepper
2 cloves garlic
4 quarts water
1 tablespoon salt

◆ Heat potatoes and enough water to cover to boiling. Cover and boil about 30 minutes or until tender; drain and cool slightly. Pare and mash potatoes; cool. Stir in 1 teaspoon salt, the eggs and enough flour to form a stiff dough. Shape into 1-inch balls.

Place remaining ingredients except water and 1 tablespoon salt in blender container. Cover and blend on medium speed until smooth.

Heat water and 1 tablespoon salt to boiling; add half of the gnocchi. After gnocchi rise to surface, boil uncovered 4 minutes. Remove with slotted spoon; drain. Repeat with remaining gnocchi. Mix gnocchi and parsley mixture.

POTATO GNOCCHI WITH SALAD

Gnocchi Spruzzati in Insalata

6 SERVINGS

1 medium baking potato (about
  6 ounces)
¼ cup crumbled Gorgonzola or
  blue cheese
½ teaspoon chopped fresh mint
1 jumbo egg
1 to 1¼ cups all-purpose flour
4 quarts water
1 tablespoon salt
1 head Boston lettuce
4 fresh pear-shaped tomatoes,
  sliced
½ cup butter, melted
½ cup extra-virgin olive oil
¼ cup freshly grated Parmesan
  cheese
1 tablespoon chopped fresh mint

◆ Heat potato and enough water to cover to boiling. Cover and boil about 30 minutes or until tender; drain and cool slightly. Pare and mash potato; cool. Stir in Gorgonzola cheese, ½ teaspoon mint, the egg and enough flour to form a stiff dough. Shape into 1-inch balls.

Heat water and salt to boiling; add gnocchi. After gnocchi rise to surface, boil uncovered 4 minutes. Remove with slotted spoon; drain.

Arrange lettuce leaves and tomatoes on serving plate; place gnocchi on top. Mix butter, oil, Parmesan cheese and 1 tablespoon mint; pour over gnocchi, tomatoes and lettuce. Serve at room temperature.

ORIENTAL SPICE GNOCCHI

Gnocchi alle Spezie Orientali   *6 SERVINGS*

2 medium baking potatoes
  (about 6 ounces each)
2 jumbo eggs
1 teaspoon freshly grated
  Parmesan cheese
½ teaspoon curry powder
2 to 2⅓ cups all-purpose flour
½ cup olive oil
3 tablespoons butter
2 tablespoons brandy
½ teaspoon curry powder
½ teaspoon green peppercorns,
  crushed
1 medium onion, thinly sliced
½ pound chicken livers, cut up
4 quarts water
1 tablespoon salt
¼ cup freshly grated Parmesan
  cheese

◆ Heat potatoes and enough water to cover to boiling. Cover and boil about 30 minutes or until tender; drain and cool slightly. Pare and mash potatoes; cool. Stir in eggs, 1 teaspoon cheese, ½ teaspoon curry powder and enough flour to form a stiff dough. Shape into 1-inch balls.

Cook oil, butter, brandy, ½ teaspoon curry powder, the peppercorns, onion and livers in 10-inch skillet over medium heat 10 to 15 minutes, stirring frequently, until livers are no longer pink inside.

Heat water and salt to boiling in Dutch oven; add half of the gnocchi. After gnocchi rise to surface, boil uncovered 4 minutes. Remove with slotted spoon; drain. Repeat with remaining gnocchi. Mix gnocchi and liver mixture; sprinkle with ¼ cup Parmesan cheese.

GNOCCHI

Until the sixteenth century, gnocchi were made with flour, eggs and water. After the discovery of the potato in America and its introduction to Italy, this nutritious vegetable became an integral ingredient of gnocchi. Potatoes were easier to grow than grain and more tolerant of the cold climate in northern Italy, and so became a staple of the northern diet. Basic gnocchi are made with potatoes, flour and eggs, to which spinach, cheeses and herbs—sometimes even meat—can be added.

FILLED RICE FRITTERS

Suppli al Telefono

ABOUT **48** FRITTERS

5 cups Chicken Broth (page 17)

2 cups uncooked Arborio rice

2 eggs, beaten

¼ cup freshly grated Parmesan cheese

1 tablespoon butter

48 cubes mozzarella cheese, each ½ inch

¼ cup ¼-inch cubes prosciutto or fully cooked Virginia ham

¼ cup ¼-inch cubes fresh mushrooms

1 cup Italian-style dry bread crumbs

Vegetable oil

◆ Heat Chicken Broth and rice to boiling; reduce heat. Cover and simmer about 20 minutes or until liquid is absorbed (do not lift cover or stir); cool. Mix eggs, rice, Parmesan cheese and butter. Shape into 1½-inch balls. Press 1 cube mozzarella cheese, 1 cube prosciutto and 1 cube mushroom in center of each ball; reshape to cover cubes completely. Roll balls in bread crumbs to coat.

Heat oil (2 inches) in deep fryer or Dutch oven to 375°. Fry 5 or 6 fritters at a time 2 minutes or until deep golden brown; drain on paper towels.

When you cut into these fritters, the melted cheese pulls into threads that look like telephone cords. That's how the dish got the name in Rome of suppli al telefono (telephone cord).

CHEESE-FILLED RICE FRITTERS

Crochette di Riso

ABOUT **60** FRITTERS

5 cups water

1 tablespoon salt

2 cups uncooked Arborio rice

4 eggs, beaten

1 cup shredded mozzarella cheese (4 ounces)

¼ cup freshly grated Parmesan cheese

Vegetable oil

◆ Heat water, salt and rice to boiling; reduce heat. Cover and simmer about 20 minutes or until liquid is absorbed (do not lift cover or stir); cool.

Mix rice, eggs and cheeses. Shape into 1½-inch balls. Heat oil (2 inches) in deep fryer or Dutch oven to 375°. Fry 5 or 6 fritters at a time about 4 minutes or until golden brown; drain on paper towels.

Filled Rice Fritters

EGGPLANT CANNELLONI

Cannelloni di Melanzane

6 SERVINGS

Orvieto in Umbria

2 large eggplant (about 1½
 pounds each)
¼ cup butter
½ cup all-purpose flour
1 teaspoon salt
½ teaspoon pepper
2 cups milk
½ cup freshly grated Parmesan
 cheese
3 tablespoons shredded Swiss
 cheese
2 egg yolks
Vegetable oil
1 cup all-purpose flour
18 thin slices prosciutto or fully
 cooked Virginia ham
¼ cup freshly grated Parmesan
 cheese

◆ Pare eggplant; cut each lengthwise into 9 slices, ¼ to ½ inch thick. Place eggplant on cutting board; sprinkle both sides with salt. Tilt board slightly; let stand 30 minutes.

Heat butter in 2-quart saucepan over medium heat. Stir in ½ cup flour, the salt and pepper. Remove from heat; gradually stir in milk. Heat to boiling, stirring constantly; boil and stir 1 minute. Remove from heat; stir in ½ cup Parmesan cheese, the Swiss cheese and egg yolks.

Heat oven to 350°. Grease rectangular pan, 13 × 9 × 2 inches. Heat oil (1 inch) in deep fryer or Dutch oven to 375°. Rinse eggplant; pat dry. Coat eggplant with 1 cup flour. Shake off excess. Fry 1 or 2 eggplant slices at a time 1 minute, turning once; drain on paper towels.

Spread each slice eggplant with 1 tablespoon sauce; top with 1 slice prosciutto. Roll up, beginning at narrow end; place seam side down in pan. Spoon remaining sauce over rolls; sprinkle with ¼ cup Parmesan cheese. Bake uncovered 20 minutes or until hot.

TIROLEAN DUMPLINGS

Canederli alla Tirolese

6 SERVINGS

1½ cups dried garbanzo beans

1 can (14½ ounces) ready-to-
serve beef broth*

½ pound sliced lean bacon, cut
into ½-inch pieces

1 medium onion, thinly sliced

2 tablespoons butter

3 to 4 slices hard-crusted Italian
bread, torn into ½-inch
pieces

¼ cup milk

½ teaspoon pepper

¼ to ½ cup all-purpose flour

4 quarts water

1 tablespoon salt

1 tablespoon chopped fresh
parsley

♦ Pour enough water over garbanzo beans to cover 2 inches above beans. Let stand at least 8 hours; drain.

Heat broth and beans to boiling; reduce heat. Cover and simmer about 30 minutes or until beans are tender.

Cook bacon and onion in butter over medium heat until bacon is crisp. Drain, reserving ¼ cup fat. Mix reserved fat and enough bread to absorb fat. Mix in bacon mixture, milk, pepper and enough flour to make stiff. Shape into 1-inch balls.

Heat water and salt to boiling in Dutch oven. Add dumplings; boil about 12 minutes or until tender. Remove with slotted spoon; drain. Mix dumplings and garbanzo beans. Sprinkle with parsley.

*1¾ cups Beef Broth (page 16) can be substituted for canned beef broth.

Tirolean Dumplings are a traditional dumpling made in the Alps. They are found in Austrian, Swiss, French and German cooking, as well as this northern Italian dish.

SAVORY ITALIAN OMELET

Frittata Aromatica

6 SERVINGS

7 jumbo eggs

¼ cup diced prosciutto or fully
  cooked Virginia ham (about
  2 ounces)

1 tablespoon chopped fresh
  basil

1 tablespoon chopped fresh
  sage

1 tablespoon chopped fresh
  mint

1 tablespoon freshly grated
  Parmesan cheese

1 teaspoon salt

½ teaspoon pepper

2 tablespoons butter

1 small onion, finely chopped
  (about ¼ cup)

◆ Beat all ingredients except butter and onion thoroughly. Heat butter in 12-inch nonstick skillet over medium-high heat. Sauté onion in butter.

Reduce heat to medium low. Stir onion mixture into egg mixture. Pour into skillet. Cook uncovered, gently lifting edge so uncooked portion can flow to bottom, until eggs are almost set and golden brown on bottom. Place 12-inch, or larger, plate over skillet; invert omelet onto plate. Slide omelet back into skillet. Cook until eggs are set and golden brown on bottom.

TRIPE WITH PARMESAN CHEESE

Trippa alla Parmigiana

6 SERVINGS

2 quarts water

1 tablespoon salt

2 pounds parboiled tripe

1 tablespoon chopped fresh
  parsley

½ pound sliced lean bacon, cut
  into ½-inch pieces

4 cloves garlic, finely chopped

1 medium onion, chopped

1 tablespoon olive oil

2 cups tomato puree

½ cup freshly grated Parmesan
  cheese

½ teaspoon pepper

◆ Heat water and salt to boiling in 4-quart Dutch oven. Add tripe. Heat to boiling; reduce heat. Cover and simmer 1 to 1½ hours or until tender; drain. Cut tripe into 2 × ½-inch strips. Cook parsley, bacon, garlic and onion in oil in 10-inch skillet over medium heat until bacon is crisp. Drain, reserving ¼ cup fat in skillet.

Add tripe, bacon mixture and tomato puree to fat in skillet. Heat to boiling; reduce heat. Simmer uncovered 20 minutes, stirring occasionally, until thickened. Stir in cheese and pepper.

FRITTATA

An Italian frittata is an open-face omelet. It is not folded like a French omelet and the ingredients are cooked with the eggs instead of being folded inside the eggs. To make a perfect frittata:

1. Sauté the ingredients for the filling in a separate pan. Cool them and fold into the eggs.

2. After pouring the frittata mixture into a hot skillet, cook until the bottom of the mixture is golden brown and the top almost firm.

3. Quickly invert the frittata onto a plate that is large enough to hold it. Slide the frittata back into the pan to brown the other side. The golden crust on the top surface keeps the inside of the frittata moist.

Savory Italian Omelet

CHAPTER FIVE

Pizza and Breads

Classic Four-Seasons
Pizza (page 106)
Above: Umbrian landscape

PIZZA

For Italians, pizza is an extension of bread. Pizza in some form has always been present throughout most of Italian history, and every region has its favorite variations. In a bakery shop in the ruins of Pompeii, archeologists found evidence of a flat bread topped with garum—a fish-and-spice paste—that was a form of pizza. Flat bread was also a staple for the Roman armies. Today, open-face pizzas, stuffed calzones and filled focaccias show the delicious evolution of pizza from a bread to a meal.

BASIC PIZZA DOUGH

Pasta per Pizze

One Crust

1 package active dry yeast
½ cup warm water (105° to 115°)
1¼ to 1½ cups all-purpose flour
1 teaspoon olive oil
½ teaspoon salt
¼ teaspoon sugar

Two Crusts

2 packages active dry yeast
1 cup warm water (105° to 115°)
2⅓ to 2⅔ cups all-purpose flour
2 teaspoons olive oil
1 teaspoon salt
½ teaspoon sugar

Three Crusts

2 packages active dry yeast
1½ cups warm water (105° to 115°)
3¾ to 4 cups all-purpose flour
1 tablespoon olive oil
1 teaspoon salt
½ teaspoon sugar

◆ Dissolve yeast in warm water in large bowl. Stir in half of the flour, the oil, salt and sugar. Stir in enough of the remaining flour to make dough easy to handle. Turn dough onto lightly floured surface; knead about 10 minutes or until smooth and elastic. Place in greased bowl; turn greased side up. Cover and let rise in warm place 20 minutes.

Punch down dough. Cover and refrigerate at least 2 hours but no longer than 48 hours. (Punch down dough as necessary.)

BASIC PIZZA

Pizza Tradizionale

2 SERVINGS

Basic Pizza Dough for One Crust (page 104)
½ cup Simple Pizza Sauce (page 83)

◆ Prepare Basic Pizza Dough and Simple Pizza Sauce. Press or roll dough from center to edge into 12-inch circle on lightly floured surface. (For Two Crusts, divide dough in half; for Three Crusts, divide dough into thirds.) Place on ungreased pizza screen or in 12-inch perforated pizza pan. Press dough from center to edge so edge is thicker than center.

Place oven rack in lowest position of oven. Heat oven to 500°. Spread pizza sauce over dough to within ½ inch of edge. Top with cheese and favorite pizza toppings. Bake 8 to 10 minutes or until crust is golden brown and cheese is melted.

CLASSIC PIZZA

Pizza Classica

2 SERVINGS

Basic Pizza Dough for One Crust (page 104)
½ cup Simple Pizza Sauce (page 83)
1 pound bulk Italian sausage
1 small onion, chopped (about ¼ cup)
1 tablespoon olive oil
1 cup shredded mozzarella cheese (4 ounces)
½ cup shredded provolone cheese (2 ounces)
¼ cup chopped fresh basil
½ cup chopped prosciutto or fully cooked Virginia ham (about 3 ounces)

◆ Prepare Basic Pizza Dough and Simple Pizza Sauce. Cook sausage and onion in oil over medium heat, stirring occasionally, until sausage is brown; drain.

Place oven rack in lowest position of oven. Heat oven to 500°. Press or roll dough from center to edge into 12-inch circle on lightly floured surface. Place on ungreased pizza screen or in 12-inch perforated pizza pan. Press dough from center to edge so edge is thicker than center. Spread pizza sauce over dough to within ½ inch of edge. Mix cheeses; sprinkle over sauce. Spread sausage mixture over cheeses; sprinkle with basil and prosciutto. Bake about 10 minutes or until crust is golden brown and cheeses are melted.

CLASSIC FOUR-SEASONS PIZZA

Pizza Quattro Stagioni

2 SERVINGS

The Classic Four-Seasons Pizza is an edible display of the year's seasons, with spring represented by fresh basil and chunks of tomato, summer by capers and anchovies, fall by cheese and winter by prosciutto, one of the more nourishing foods available in winter.

Basic Pizza Dough for One Crust (page 104)

½ cup Simple Pizza Sauce (page 83)

1 cup shredded mozzarella cheese (4 ounces)

⅓ cup shredded provolone cheese (about 1½ ounces)

⅓ cup chopped prosciutto or fully cooked Virginia ham (about 2 ounces)

¼ cup chopped fresh basil

2 teaspoons large capers, drained

4 marinated artichoke hearts, cut into fourths

4 flat fillets of anchovy in oil

3 fresh pear-shaped tomatoes, peeled and chopped*

1 teaspoon olive oil

12 imported Italian black olives, pitted

♦ Prepare Basic Pizza Dough and Simple Pizza Sauce.

Place oven rack in lowest position of oven. Heat oven to 500°. Press or roll dough into 12-inch circle on lightly floured surface. Place on ungreased pizza screen or in 12-inch perforated pizza pan. Press dough from center to edge so edge is thicker than center. Spread pizza sauce over dough to within ½ inch of edge. Mix cheeses; sprinkle over sauce. Place prosciutto, basil, capers, artichoke hearts, fillets of anchovy and tomatoes on cheeses; drizzle with oil. Place olives on top.

Bake 8 to 10 minutes or until crust is golden and cheeses are melted.

*3 canned imported pear-shaped tomatoes, drained, can be substituted for the fresh tomatoes.

SEAFOOD PIZZA

Pizza Marinara

2 SERVINGS

Basic Pizza Dough for One
    Crust (page 104)
I cup Simple Pizza Sauce (page
    83)
12 medium raw shrimp in shells
I cup shredded mozzarella
    cheese (4 ounces)
½ cup shredded provolone
    cheese (2 ounces)
8 flat fillets of anchovy in oil
½ pound bay scallops
½ cup chopped fresh basil
½ teaspoon pepper
4 cloves garlic, finely chopped

◆ Prepare Basic Pizza Dough and Simple Pizza
Sauce.

Place oven rack in lowest position of oven.
Heat oven to 500°. Peel shrimp, leaving tails
intact. Press or roll dough into 12-inch circle on
lightly floured surface. Place on ungreased pizza
screen or in 12-inch perforated pizza pan. Press
dough from center to edge so edge is thicker
than center. Spread pizza sauce over dough to
within ½ inch of edge. Mix cheeses; sprinkle
over sauce. Place shrimp, fillets of anchovy and
scallops on cheeses. Mix basil, pepper and garlic;
sprinkle over seafood. Bake about 10 minutes or
until seafood is done and cheeses are melted.

PIZZA PIE WITH BASIL-GARLIC SAUCE

Pesto Focaccia

4 SERVINGS

Basic Pizza Dough for Two
    Crusts (page 104)
Basil Garlic Sauce (page 85)
I egg, beaten
4 cups shredded mozzarella
    cheese (16 ounces)
2 cups shredded provolone
    cheese (8 ounces)
8 ounces fresh mushrooms, thinly
    sliced
I medium onion, thinly sliced
½ pound thinly sliced Genoa
    salami

◆ Prepare Basic Pizza Dough and Basil-Garlic
Sauce.

Heat oven to 375°. Grease 2 cookie sheets.
Divide dough into 4 equal parts. Press or roll
one part dough into 12-inch circle on cookie
sheet; brush ½-inch edge of dough with egg.
Arrange half of the cheeses, mushrooms, onion
and salami on circle to within ½ inch of edge.
Spread with half of the sauce.

Press or roll one part dough into 12-inch circle
on lightly floured surface; place over filling. Press
edges of dough together with fingers or fork to
seal; prick top of dough thoroughly with fork.
Brush top with egg. Repeat with remaining parts
dough and remaining ingredients. Bake about
30 minutes or until golden brown. (If necessary,
refrigerate one pizza while other bakes.)

RUSTIC PIZZA PIE

Pizza Rustica (Focaccia)

4 SERVINGS

Basic Pizza Dough for Two
  Crusts (page 104)
1 cup Simple Pizza Sauce (page
  83)
½ pound bulk Italian sausage,
  cooked and drained
1 cup shredded mozzarella
  cheese (4 ounces)
½ cup shredded provolone
  cheese (2 ounces)
½ cup sliced fresh mushrooms
½ cup chopped Genoa salami
  (about 3 ounces)
1 medium onion, sliced
1 cup chopped fresh basil
1 tablespoon extra-virgin olive
  oil
1 egg, beaten

◆ Prepare Basic Pizza Dough and Simple Pizza Sauce.

Heat oven to 425°. Grease pie plate, 10 × 1½ inches. Divide dough in half. Press or roll one half into 13-inch circle on lightly floured surface; place in pie plate. Sprinkle sausage over dough in pie plate. Mix cheeses; sprinkle over sausage. Top with Simple Pizza Sauce, mushrooms, salami, onion and basil; drizzle with oil.

Press or roll remaining dough into 11-inch circle on lightly floured surface; place over filling. Pinch edges of dough together to seal; roll edge of dough up, forming a rim. Prick top of dough thoroughly with fork; brush with egg. Bake about 30 minutes or until golden brown. Serve hot or cold.

Rustic Pizza pies, or focaccias, come from rural southern Italy. They were prepared for holidays throughout the year and reflect the religious laws of the Catholic church. Sfinciuni, a Sicilian focaccia, is filled with seafood, eggs and vegetables during Lent when meat is prohibited, but it can be filled with meat—or sometimes small birds—the rest of the year. Focaccias are baked at a moderate heat to allow the ingredients inside to cook evenly, unlike pizza, which is cooked quickly at a high temperature.

Rustic Pizza Pie

SAVORY BASIL AND CHEESE PIZZA PIE, GENOA-STYLE

Torta alla Genovese

8 SERVINGS

Basic Pizza Dough for Two
    Crusts (page 104)
2 medium carrots, chopped
    (about 1 cup)
1 small onion, chopped (about
    ¼ cup)
1 pound bulk Italian sausage
1 tablespoon butter
1 egg white
2 eggs
8 ounces fresh basil, torn into
    small pieces (about 5½
    cups)*
5 cups shredded mozzarella
    cheese (20 ounces)
1 egg yolk

♦ Prepare Basic Pizza Dough. Cook carrots, onion and sausage in butter over medium heat, stirring frequently, until sausage is brown and carrot is tender; drain. Mix sausage mixture, egg white, 2 eggs, the basil and cheese.

Place oven rack in lowest position of oven. Heat oven to 425°. Grease round pan, 9 × 1½ inches. Divide dough in half. Press or roll one half dough into 13-inch circle on lightly floured surface; place in pan. Spoon filling onto dough in pan. Press or roll remaining dough into 11-inch circle on lightly floured surface; place over filling. Pinch edges of dough together to seal; roll edge of dough, forming a rim.

Beat egg yolk; brush over top of dough. Cut slits in top. Bake 25 minutes; cover top with aluminum foil to prevent excessive browning. Bake 25 minutes longer; remove from pan.

*8 ounces fresh spinach, torn into small pieces, can be substituted for the basil.

PIZZA FOLDOVER

Calzone

1 OR 2 SERVINGS

Basic Pizza Dough for One
  Crust (page 104)
1/3 cup Simple Pizza Sauce (page
  83)
1/2 cup shredded mozzarella
  cheese (2 ounces)
1/4 cup shredded provolone
  cheese (1 ounce)
1/3 cup chopped prosciutto or fully
  cooked Virginia ham (about
  2 ounces)
1/3 cup chopped Genoa salami
  (about 2 ounces)
2 tablespoons chopped fresh
  basil

◆ Prepare Basic Pizza Dough and Simple Pizza Sauce.

Heat oven to 475°. Grease cookie sheet. Press or roll dough from center to edge into 12-inch circle on cookie sheet. Mix cheeses; place in center of circle. (Keep edge of circle clean to ensure secure seal.) Mix prosciutto and salami; sprinkle over cheeses. Pour pizza sauce over prosciutto and salami; sprinkle with basil. Lift and gently stretch dough over filling; press edges of dough together with fingers or fork to seal. Cut slit in top. Bake about 10 minutes or until golden brown.

A calzone is like a folded-over stuffed pizza; the circle of the dough is folded in half over the filling, then sealed. During baking the filling plumps, stretching the dough somewhat until it resembles a "stuffed stocking," the literal translation of calzone.

VOLCANO-FOLDOVER PIZZA

Stromboli Ripieno

6 SERVINGS

Basic Pizza Dough for Three
  Crusts (page 104)
2 tablespoons butter
4 cloves garlic, finely chopped
2 medium green bell peppers,
  chopped (about 2 cups)
1 medium onion, chopped
  (about 1/2 cup)
1 pound bulk Italian sausage
4 cups shredded mozzarella
  cheese (16 ounces)
2 cups shredded Asiago cheese
  (8 ounces)
1/2 teaspoon pepper
12 cherry tomatoes, cut in half

◆ Prepare Basic Pizza Dough. Heat butter in 10-inch skillet over medium heat. Sauté garlic, bell peppers, and onion in butter. Stir in sausage. Cook, stirring frequently, until sausage is brown; drain. Refrigerate sausage mixture until cool.

Heat oven to 350°. Grease 3 cookie sheets. Stir cheeses, pepper and tomatoes into sausage mixture. Divide dough into thirds. Press or roll each third into 12-inch circle on cookie sheet. Spoon 1/3 of the filling onto center of each circle. (Keep edge of circle clean to ensure secure seal.) Lift and gently stretch dough over filling; press edges of dough together with fingers or fork to seal. Cut 2 slits in top of each. Bake about 30 minutes or until golden brown. (If necessary, refrigerate one or two foldover pizzas while others bake.)

Following pages: Pizza Foldover, Volcano-Foldover Pizza

BAKING BREAD

Before the days of mass production, it was the common practice for small loaves of bread to be baked daily by professional bakers, and for Italian women to take them home in cloth-covered baskets. There was religious significance to the baking of the bread—the slits on the top of the bread were a tribute to God for leavening the dough, the loaves' white dusting of flour a thanks for supplying bread in harsh, sometimes snowy winters and the cornmeal often found on the bottom a reminder of the summer's bountiful days.

WHITE BREAD

Pane Bianco

I LOAF

4 packages active dry yeast
I cup warm water (105° to 115°)
I cup warm milk (105° to 115°)
5½ to 6 cups bread flour or all-purpose flour
I tablespoon salt
I tablespoon butter, softened
I teaspoon sugar

◆ Dissolve yeast in warm water in large bowl. Stir in milk, 4 cups of the flour, the salt, butter and sugar. Stir in enough of the remaining flour to make dough easy to handle. Turn dough onto lightly floured surface; knead 5 minutes. Cover and let rest 20 minutes.

Knead dough on lightly floured surface about 10 minutes or until smooth and elastic. Place in greased bowl; turn greased side up. Cover and let rise in warm place about 45 minutes or until double. (Dough is ready if indentation remains when touched.)

Grease cookie sheet. Punch down dough; roll into rectangle, 14 × 10 inches. Roll up tightly, beginning at 10-inch side. Pinch edge of dough into roll to seal well. Roll gently back and forth to taper ends. Place seam side down on cookie sheet. Cover and let rise in warm place 30 minutes or until double.

Heat oven to 325°. Make 3 slashes, about ¼ inch deep, across loaf; dust with flour. Bake about 55 minutes or until golden brown and loaf sounds hollow when tapped.

HOMEMADE MILK BREAD

Pane al Latte

4 LOAVES

4 cups bread flour or all-
  purpose flour
1⅓ cups semolina flour
1 tablespoon salt
3 packages active dry yeast
½ cup firm butter
2 cups very warm milk (120°
  to 130°)
1 egg, beaten
½ teaspoon kosher salt
½ teaspoon cumin seed

◆ Mix flours. Place 3 cups of the flour mixture in large bowl; stir in 1 tablespoon salt and the yeast. Cut butter into the 3 cups flour mixture; stir in milk. Stir in enough of the remaining flour mixture to make dough easy to handle. (Stir in additional bread flour if necessary.) Turn dough onto lightly floured surface; knead 5 minutes or until smooth and elastic. (Dough should feel soft and moist but not sticky.) Place in greased bowl; dust with flour. Cover and let rise in warm place 30 minutes or until double.

Dust 2 cookie sheets with flour. Punch down dough; turn onto lightly floured surface. Knead 5 minutes. Pat dough into 12-inch square; cut into 4 triangles. Place 2 triangles on each cookie sheet. Cover and let rise in warm place 45 minutes or until double.

Heat oven to 325°. Brush loaves with egg; sprinkle with kosher salt and cumin. Bake about 50 minutes or until deep golden brown. (If necessary, refrigerate 2 loaves while first 2 bake.)

Doorway in Populonia, Tuscany

This Sweet Bread Wreath shows the versatility of pizza dough. Here it is sweetened, spiced and braided to form a wreath. You can also form the dough into other shapes—a heart, an animal—whatever appeals to you.

SWEET BREAD WREATH

Corona Dolce

1 WREATH

Basic Pizza Dough for Three Crusts (page 104)
2 eggs, beaten
¼ cup sugar
½ teaspoon ground cinnamon
½ teaspoon ground anise
¼ teaspoon freshly grated nutmeg

◆ Prepare Basic Pizza Dough.

Heat oven to 350°. Grease cookie sheet. Divide dough into thirds. Roll each third dough into rope, 26 inches long. Braid ropes gently and loosely; pinch ends together. Shape braid into wreath on cookie sheet; pinch ends together. Let rise in warm place about 1 hour or until double.

Brush wreath with eggs. Mix remaining ingredients; sprinkle on wreath. Bake 25 to 30 minutes or until golden brown.

Sweet Bread Wreath

FLORENTINE ROSEMARY BREAD

Pan di Ramerino di Firenze

6 LOAVES

Before the sixteenth century, this bread was eaten as a dessert, with honey having been mixed into the dough. As sugar became more readily available, allowing Florentine bakers to create dessert cakes, this herb bread became an accompaniment, not an end, to the meal.

3 packages active dry yeast
1½ cups warm water (105° to 115°)
3 cups bread flour or all-purpose flour
¼ cup olive oil
1 tablespoon golden raisins
1 tablespoon chopped fresh rosemary
1 tablespoon sugar
1 teaspoon salt
1 egg white, beaten

◆ Dissolve yeast in warm water in large bowl. Stir in 2 cups of the flour. Stir in enough of the remaining flour to make dough easy to handle. Turn dough onto lightly floured surface; knead about 10 minutes or until smooth and elastic. Place in greased bowl; sprinkle with flour. Cover and let rise in warm place 50 to 60 minutes or until double.

Heat oil over medium-high heat. Sauté raisins and rosemary in oil; cool. Grease 2 cookie sheets. Punch down dough. Turn dough onto lightly floured surface; knead in raisin mixture, sugar and salt until evenly distributed. Divide dough into 6 equal parts. Shape each part into 3-inch round on cookie sheet. Cover and let rise in warm place 20 to 30 minutes or until double.

Heat oven to 325°. Cut an X shape about ¼ inch deep in top of each round. Bake 30 minutes; brush with egg white. Bake about 10 minutes or until deep golden brown and loaves sound hollow when tapped. (If necessary, refrigerate 3 loaves while first 3 bake.)

SPICY BREADSTICKS

Grissini Piccanti

24 BREADSTICKS

Basic Pizza Dough for Three
    Crusts (page 104)
1 tablespoon freshly grated
    Parmesan cheese
1 tablespoon freshly grated Ro-
    mano cheese
1 teaspoon dried oregano
1 teaspoon dried basil
½ teaspoon garlic salt
½ teaspoon pepper

◆ Prepare Basic Pizza Dough.

Heat oven to 350°. Grease 2 cookie sheets. Press or roll dough into rectangle, 24 × 12 inches. Mix remaining ingredients; sprinkle evenly over dough. Gently press herb mixture into dough.

Cut dough into 24 strips, 12 × 1 inch; place strips ½ inch apart on cookie sheets. Bake about 10 minutes or until golden brown.

*Villa garden
in Capri*

CHAPTER SIX

Seafood

*Grilled Salmon with Mint
Marinade (page 125)
Above: Gondolas along the
Piazza San Marco, Venice*

MEDITERRANEAN-STYLE SOLE

Sogliole alla Mediterranea   *4 SERVINGS*

4 sole fillets (about 1¼ pounds)
½ cup all-purpose flour
2 eggs, beaten
1 cup Italian-style dry bread
   crumbs
1 tablespoon chopped fresh
   sage
1 tablespoon chopped fresh
   rosemary
¼ cup butter
½ cup dry white wine
3 tablespoons lemon juice

◆ Pat sole fillets dry. Coat fish with flour; dip into eggs. Coat with bread crumbs.

Cook sage and rosemary in butter in 12-inch skillet over low heat, stirring occasionally, 6 minutes. Add fish; cook uncovered over medium heat 4 minutes. Turn fish carefully. Add wine and lemon juice. Cook about 5 minutes longer or until fish flakes easily with fork.

FILLET OF SOLE, PARMA-STYLE

Sogliole alla Parmigiana   *4 SERVINGS*

2 green onions (with tops),
   thinly sliced
¼ cup butter
8 sole fillets (about 2½
   pounds)
1 cup all-purpose flour
½ teaspoon salt
½ teaspoon pepper
1 cup dry white wine
3 tablespoons lemon juice
1 cup freshly grated Parmesan
   cheese
Parsley sprigs

◆ Heat oven to 375°. Cook onions in butter in 12-inch ovenproof skillet over medium-low heat 5 minutes. Coat sole fillets with flour; place in skillet. Cook uncovered 4 minutes; turn carefully. Cook 4 minutes longer.

Sprinkle fish with salt and pepper. Add wine and lemon juice; sprinkle with cheese. Bake uncovered 15 minutes or until hot and bubbly. Garnish with parsley.

COD WITH POTATOES IN CREAM SAUCE

Baccala alle Patate e Olive

4 SERVINGS

1 pound boneless salt cod
3 tablespoons butter, softened
1 pound red potatoes, pared
    and sliced
4 cups milk
1 cup whipping (heavy) cream
½ teaspoon salt
½ teaspoon pepper
½ teaspoon paprika
1 cup sliced green olives

◆ Place salt cod in large bowl; cover with water. Cover and refrigerate at least 12 hours, changing water 2 or 3 times.

Spread butter in 12-inch skillet. Cut cod into 2 × 1-inch slices. Alternate layers of cod and potatoes in skillet. Pour milk and whipping cream over cod and potatoes; sprinkle with salt, pepper and paprika. Heat to boiling; reduce heat to medium-low. Cover and simmer 45 minutes. Carefully stir in olives. Cover and cook 10 minutes longer.

Salt cod, imported from Scandinavian countries, has been eaten for centuries in Italy, especially during Lent, a time when meat is prohibited by Catholic church law. Salt cod, preserved with large amounts of salt, must first be soaked in water before cooking—as in this recipe for Cod with Potatoes in Cream Sauce.

MULLET WITH BELL PEPPER AND PARSLEY SAUCE

Triglie al Verde

4 SERVINGS

2 green onions (with tops),
    chopped
1 green bell pepper, cut into
    1 × ½-inch strips
2 tablespoons chopped fresh
    parsley
¼ cup olive oil
8 pan-dressed mullet (½ to ¾
    pound each)
1 cup dry white wine
2 tablespoons lemon juice
½ teaspoon salt
½ teaspoon pepper

◆ Cook onions, bell pepper and parsley in oil in 12-inch skillet over medium-low heat 8 minutes. Place mullet on top of vegetables and add remaining ingredients. Cover and cook over medium heat 25 minutes or until fish flakes easily with fork.

Mullet, called triglie in Italy, are considered a delicacy, especially when they are prepared Livornese style as they are here, with a parsley and lemon sauce. Small mullet are excellent for stews, and one-pound mullet are good for grilling.

BAKED ROCKFISH

Branzino al Forno

4 SERVINGS

½ cup Basil-Garlic Sauce (page 85)
3 tablespoons lemon juice
1 carrot, chopped
1 leek, chopped
2 tablespoons firm butter
1 drawn rockfish or red snapper (about 2 pounds)

◆ Heat oven to 375°. Mix Basil-Garlic Sauce, lemon juice, carrot and leek. Cut butter into small pieces. Place in rectangular baking dish, 13 × 9 × 2 inches. Place rockfish on butter. Spread vegetable mixture over fish. Cover and bake 40 minutes or until fish flakes easily with fork.

GRILLED SALMON WITH MINT MARINADE

Salmone Marinato alla Menta

4 SERVINGS

4 small salmon steaks, ¾ inch thick (about 1½ pounds)
½ cup chopped fresh mint
½ cup olive oil
3 tablespoons lemon juice
½ teaspoon salt
½ teaspoon pepper
1 clove garlic, finely chopped
1 bay leaf

◆ Place salmon steaks in ungreased rectangular baking dish, 11 × 7 × 1½ inches. Beat remaining ingredients except bay leaf thoroughly; stir in bay leaf and drizzle over fish. Cover and refrigerate 1 hour, turning fish over after 30 minutes. Remove fish from marinade; reserve marinade.

Grill fish uncovered about 4 inches from hot coals, turning over once and brushing with marinade frequently, 10 to 15 minutes or until fish flakes easily with fork. Heat remaining marinade to rolling boil; remove bay leaf. Serve marinade with fish.

BROILED SALMON WITH MINT MARINADE: Marinate fish as directed above. Set oven control to broil. Place fish on rack in broiler pan. Broil with tops about 4 inches from heat about 5 minutes, brushing fish with marinade frequently, until light brown. Turn carefully; brush with marinade. Broil 4 to 6 minutes longer, brushing with marinade frequently, until fish flakes easily with fork.

GRILLING FISH

Grilling is a popular and delicious method of preparing fish. For successful grilling:

1. Clean the grill thoroughly and grease the gridiron with olive oil.

2. After cleaning fish, coat with salted cornmeal to prevent fish from sticking to the grill.

3. Raise the gridiron as high as possible above the heat source to prevent flames from reaching the fish and causing uneven cooking.

Baked Rockfish

STUFFED SEA BASS
Persico Ripieno

4 *SERVINGS*

1 cup seasoned croutons
1 cup sliced fresh mushrooms
½ cup dry white wine
1 tablespoon chopped fresh
parsley
1 tablespoon chopped fresh
basil
½ teaspoon salt
½ teaspoon pepper
1 clove garlic, finely chopped
1 egg
1 dressed sea bass (about 2
pounds)
½ cup olive oil

◆ Heat oven to 350°. Mix all ingredients except sea bass and oil. Cut 3 diagonal slits on
each side of fish. Place 1 tablespoon stuffing
mixture in each slit; fill cavity of fish with
remaining stuffing mixture. Place fish in ungreased rectangular baking dish, 12 × 7½ × 2
inches; drizzle with oil. Bake uncovered 30 to
40 minutes or until fish flakes easily with fork.

GOLDEN FRIED TROUT
Torte Fritte

4 *SERVINGS*

4 pan-dressed rainbow trout
(about 1 pound each)
½ cup dry white wine
3 tablespoons lemon juice
1 jumbo egg
1 cup all-purpose flour
1 cup Italian-style dry bread
crumbs
Vegetable oil
1 lemon, sliced
Parsley sprigs

◆ To butterfly, cut each trout lengthwise almost in half, leaving skin along back intact.
Open fish to lie flat.

Beat wine, lemon juice and egg. Coat fish with
flour; dip into wine mixture. Press bread crumbs
on open cut side of each fish.

Heat oil (2 inches) in Dutch oven to 375°.
Fry 2 fish at a time, 2 to 3 minutes on each
side or until golden brown. Serve with lemon
and parsley.

Stuffed Sea Bass

GRILLED SWORDFISH
Pesce Spada alla Griglia

4 SERVINGS

*Sardinian
coastline, near
Santa Margherita*

½ cup olive oil
2 tablespoons capers, drained
2 tablespoons lemon juice
1 tablespoon chopped fresh
  parsley
½ teaspoon pepper
2 flat fillets of anchovy in oil
2 cloves garlic
4 swordfish steaks, about 1
  inch thick (about 2 pounds)

◆ Place all ingredients except swordfish steaks in food processor or in blender; cover and process until smooth. Place fish in ungreased rectangular baking dish, 12 × 7½ × 2 inches. Pour oil mixture over fish. Cover and refrigerate 1 hour, turning fish after 30 minutes.

Grill fish uncovered about 4 inches from hot coals, turning once and brushing with marinade occasionally, 10 to 15 minutes or until fish flakes easily with fork.

BROILED SWORDFISH: Marinade fish as directed above. Set oven control to broil. Place fish on rack in broiler pan. Broil with tops about 4 inches from heat about 6 minutes; brushing fish with marinade frequently, until light brown. Turn carefully; brush with marinade. Broil 4 to 6 minutes longer, brushing with marinade, until fish flakes easily with fork.

FRESH TUNA AND PEAS
Tonno ai Piselli

6 SERVINGS

1 package (16 ounces) frozen
  green peas
¼ cup olive oil
1 small onion, finely chopped
1 clove garlic, finely chopped
1 tablespoon chopped fresh
  parsley
1 can (28 ounces) imported
  pear-shaped tomatoes
2 pounds tuna steaks, cut into
  1-inch cubes
½ teaspoon salt
½ teaspoon pepper

◆ Rinse peas under cold water to separate; drain. Heat oil in 12-inch skillet over medium-high heat. Sauté onion, garlic and parsley in oil. Stir in peas. Cook uncovered over medium heat 4 minutes. Stir in tomatoes, tuna, salt and pepper; break up tomatoes. Cover and cook 20 minutes or until fish flakes easily with fork.

MARINATED CATFISH

Lamprede Marinate

6 SERVINGS

2 cups Sugo Sauce (page 84)
6 small catfish (about ½ pound each), skinned and pan dressed
1 cup all-purpose flour
¼ cup plus 2 tablespoons olive oil
4 cups red-wine vinegar
½ teaspoon salt
½ teaspoon pepper
6 bay leaves
2 cloves garlic, finely chopped

◆ Prepare Sugo Sauce. Rinse catfish; pat dry. Coat fish with flour. Heat oil in 12-inch skillet. Cook fish in oil, turning once, until golden brown; drain on paper towels. Place fish in ungreased rectangular baking dish, 13 × 9 × 2 inches.

Mix remaining ingredients in skillet. Heat to boiling; reduce heat. Simmer uncovered 15 minutes; pour over fish. Cover and refrigerate at least 12 hours but no longer than 3 days. Remove bay leaves; serve cold.

This recipe for marinating cooked fish echoes back to the ancient Etruscans. They learned three basic ways to preserve food, which allowed them to trade goods all over the Mediterranean. They boiled food and then stored it in salt water; they spiced the food and preserved it in olive oil; or they preserved the food in vinegar or alcohol.

FLAMBÉED BOILED SHRIMP

Gamberi Bolliti alla Fiamma

4 SERVINGS

4 quarts water
1 tablespoon salt
1 pound medium raw shrimp in shells
2 green onions (with tops), thinly sliced
2 tablespoons chopped fresh sage
3 tablespoons butter
⅓ cup vodka or light rum

◆ Heat water and salt to boiling in large kettle or stockpot. Add shrimp. Cover and heat to boiling. Boil 6 to 8 minutes or until shrimp are pink and firm; drain. Let stand about 10 minutes or until shrimp are cool enough to handle. Remove shells and veins.

Cook onions and sage in butter in 10-inch skillet over medium-low heat 8 minutes. Add shrimp. Heat over high heat, stirring occasionally, until hot. Add vodka; heat 1 minute. Carefully ignite. Serve when flame dies out.

BAKED JUMBO SHRIMP

Gamberoni al Forno

4 SERVINGS

16 jumbo raw shrimp in shells
½ cup olive oil
2 tablespoons chopped fresh
    parsley
2 green onions (with tops),
    thinly sliced
2 cloves garlic, finely chopped
1 cup dry white wine
3 tablespoons lemon juice
½ teaspoon salt
½ teaspoon pepper

◆ Heat oven to 375°. Peel shrimp. Make a shallow cut lengthwise down back of each shrimp; wash out vein. Pour oil into rectangular baking dish, 13 × 9 × 2 inches. Place shrimp in oil; sprinkle with parsley, onions and garlic. Pour wine and lemon juice over shrimp; sprinkle with salt and pepper. Bake uncovered about 20 minutes or until shrimp are pink and firm.

SWEET AND SOUR SHRIMP

Gamberi in Dolceforte

4 SERVINGS

½ cup light rum
½ cup raisins
1 pound large raw shrimp in
    shells
¼ cup all-purpose flour
¼ cup olive oil
½ teaspoon salt
½ teaspoon pepper
½ teaspoon ground cinnamon
½ teaspoon curry powder
3 tablespoons lemon juice

◆ Pour rum over raisins. Let stand 30 minutes.

Peel shrimp. Make a shallow cut lengthwise down back of each shrimp; wash out vein. Pat shrimp dry; coat with flour. Heat oil in 10-inch skillet over medium-high heat. Sauté shrimp in oil until pink. Sprinkle with salt, pepper, cinnamon and curry powder; reduce heat. Stir in rum, raisins and lemon juice. Cover and simmer 8 minutes.

Baked Jumbo Shrimp,
White Bread (page 114)

CRAB LEGS WITH VINAIGRETTE

Granchi all'Aceto

6 SERVINGS

4 quarts water

1 tablespoon salt

2 pounds crab legs, sectioned
   into 2-inch pieces

2 green onions (with tops),
   thinly sliced

2 tablespoons chopped fresh
   parsley

2 tablespoons chopped fresh
   mint

3 tablespoons butter

1/4 cup Marsala or dry red wine

1/4 cup red-wine vinegar

◆ Heat water and salt to boiling in large kettle or stockpot. Add crab legs. Cover and heat to boiling; reduce heat. Simmer 10 minutes; drain. Let stand about 10 minutes or until cool enough to handle. Crack crab legs with nutcracker; remove meat with sharp knife.,

Cook onions, parsley and mint in butter in 10-inch skillet over low heat 8 minutes. Stir in crabmeat, wine and vinegar. Cook uncovered over medium heat 5 minutes.

LOBSTER WITH SPARKLING WINE SAUCE

Aragosta allo Spumante

4 SERVINGS

4 quarts water

1 tablespoon salt

4 large fresh or frozen (thawed)
   lobster tails (about 1 pound
   each)

2 tablespoons butter

6 fresh pear-shaped tomatoes,
   peeled and chopped

2 green onions (with tops),
   sliced

1 cup Asti Spumante or dry
   white wine

2 tablespoons lemon juice

◆ Heat water and salt to boiling in large kettle or stockpot. Add lobster tails. Cover and heat to boiling; reduce heat. Simmer 12 minutes; drain. Let stand about 10 minutes or until cool enough to handle. Crack shells with nutcracker; remove meat with sharp knife. Cut meat into 1-inch pieces.

Heat butter in 12-inch skillet over medium-high heat. Sauté tomatoes and onions in butter. Add lobster, wine and lemon juice. Cook uncovered over medium heat, stirring occasionally, 5 minutes or until most of the liquid is evaporated.

STEAMED MUSSELS IN WINE SAUCE

Cozze al Vino

4 SERVINGS

24 large mussels (about 2 pounds)
2 tablespoons olive oil
½ cup chopped fresh parsley
4 cloves garlic, finely chopped
1 cup dry white wine
½ teaspoon salt
½ teaspoon pepper

◆ Discard any broken-shell or open (dead) mussels. Wash remaining mussels, removing any barnacles with a dull paring knife. Remove beards by tugging them away from shells.

Heat oil in 12-inch skillet over medium-high heat. Sauté parsley and garlic in oil. Add mussels, wine, salt and pepper. Cover and cook 10 minutes. Discard unopened mussels. Drizzle liquid from skillet over each serving.

VENETIAN SCALLOPS

Pettini alla Veneziana

4 SERVINGS

1 small onion, thinly sliced
2 tablespoons butter
1 pound sea scallops
½ cup dry white wine
1 cup whipping (heavy) cream
½ teaspoon freshly grated nutmeg
½ cup Italian-style dry bread crumbs
½ cup freshly grated Parmesan cheese

◆ Heat oven to 400°. Cook onion in butter in 10-inch ovenproof skillet over medium-low heat until onion is tender. Add scallops; cook 5 minutes. Stir in wine. Cook uncovered until liquid is evaporated. Stir in whipping cream and nutmeg.

Mix bread crumbs and cheese; sprinkle over scallops. Bake uncovered 12 to 15 minutes or until hot and bubbly.

Following pages: Steamed Mussels in Wine Sauce, Homemade Milk Bread (page 115)

NEAPOLITAN CALAMARI

Calamari alla Napoletana

4 SERVINGS

Calamari—squid—is a tender and delicious mollusk, commonly served in Italy, and is becoming increasingly popular in America. Often the inner ink sac from squid is reserved and used to make a special "black sauce" for rice and pasta dishes.

1½ pounds fresh squid-tail cones (calamari)
¼ cup olive oil
4 cloves garlic, cut in half
8 fresh pear-shaped tomatoes, cut in half
½ small red chili, seeded and finely chopped
½ cup chopped walnuts
½ cup sliced green olives
¼ cup golden raisins
½ cup dry white wine
2 tablespoons chopped fresh parsley
½ teaspoon salt

◆ Wash squid and pat dry. Cut squid into ¼-inch slices. Heat oil in 10-inch skillet over medium-high heat. Sauté garlic in oil. Stir in tomatoes, chili and squid; cook uncovered 5 minutes, stirring occasionally. Stir in remaining ingredients. Heat to boiling; reduce heat to medium. Cover and cook, stirring occasionally, 20 minutes. (Do not overcook or squid will be tough.) To serve, spoon liquid from skillet over each serving.

OCTOPUS FRITTERS

Polpetti Fritti

4 SERVINGS

Octopus, popular in Italy, is most tasty when one pound or smaller. Though an octopus can become enormous —up to 25 pounds—the meat from a large octopus is tough. Octopus is delicious fried, as in this recipe, as an appetizer, in salads or in stews. When preparing octopus, always remove the ink sac and mouth before cooking.

½ cup olive oil
2 tablespoons chopped fresh rosemary
½ teaspoon salt
½ teaspoon white pepper
3 tablespoons lemon juice
1 clove garlic, finely chopped
Vegetable oil
1 pound small octopus
1 cup all-purpose flour

◆ Mix olive oil, rosemary, salt, white pepper, lemon juice and garlic; reserve.

Heat vegetable oil (2 inches) in Dutch oven to 375°. Wash and cut octopus into 2-inch pieces; pat dry. Dip octopus in flour. Fry several pieces at a time 40 seconds or until done. Remove octopus with slotted spoon; drain on paper towels. Serve with reserved olive-oil mixture.

Neapolitan Calamari

*Piazza in
San Gimignano*

GRILLED SEAFOOD KABOBS

Spiedini di Pesce Misto

4 SERVINGS

Marinade (below)
4 ounces salmon steak, cut into
    1-inch cubes
4 ounces monkfish, cut into
    1-inch cubes
4 ounces rockfish, cut into
    1-inch cubes
12 medium raw shrimp in shells
4 small squid (calamari), cleaned
8 fresh large mushroom caps
1 large red bell pepper, cut
    into 1½-inch pieces
4 green onions (with tops), cut
    into 1-inch pieces
8 fresh or dried bay leaves

◆ Prepare Marinade; reserve. Alternate fish, shrimp, squid, mushrooms, bell pepper, onions and bay leaves on each of four 12-inch metal skewers. Place kabobs in ungreased rectangular baking dish, 13 × 9 × 2 inches. Drizzle Marinade over kabobs. Cover and refrigerate 45 minutes. Remove kabobs from Marinade; reserve Marinade.

Grill kabobs uncovered about 4 inches from hot coals 10 minutes, turning once and brushing with reserved Marinade occasionally, until fish flakes easily with fork. Discard bay leaves.

Marinade

½ cup olive oil
1 tablespoon chopped fresh basil
1 tablespoon chopped
    fresh parsley
3 tablespoons lemon
    juice
1 tablespoon capers, drained
1 teaspoon freshly ground pepper
½ teaspoon salt
1 green onion (with top),
    chopped

Place all ingredients in food processor or in blender; cover and process until smooth.

BROILED SEAFOOD KABOBS: Set oven control to broil. Place kabobs on rack in broiler pan. Broil with tops about 4 inches from heat 4 minutes, brushing with Marinade occasionally. Turn kabobs; brush with Marinade. Broil about 4 minutes longer, brushing with Marinade occasionally, until fish flakes easily with fork. Discard bay leaves.

SEAFOOD STEW

Cassola di Pesce

6 SERVINGS

¼ cup olive oil

4 cloves garlic, finely chopped

1 small red chili, seeded and
   finely chopped

6 mussels

1 can (28 ounces) imported
   pear-shaped tomatoes,
   drained and chopped

6 large raw shrimp in shells

½ pound cod, halibut or sole
   fillets

4 small squid (calamari), cleaned

1 pan-dressed mackerel or mullet, cut in half (about 1
   pound)

1 salmon steak (5 to 6 ounces)

1 swordfish steak (5 to 6
   ounces)

8 cups Chicken Broth (page 17)

1 cup chopped fresh clams

½ cup dry white wine

1 tablespoon chopped fresh
   sage

◆ Heat oil in 6-quart Dutch oven over medium-high heat. Sauté garlic and chili in oil. Discard any broken-shell or open (dead) mussels. Wash remaining mussels, removing any barnacles with a dull paring knife. Remove beards by tugging them away from shells. Add mussels and tomatoes to garlic mixture; cover and cook over medium heat 5 minutes.

Peel shrimp. Make a shallow cut lengthwise down back of each shrimp; wash out vein. Add shrimp and remaining ingredients to tomato mixture. Heat to boiling; reduce heat. Cover and simmer, stirring occasionally, 1 hour. Discard unopened mussels.

In Italy and other Mediterranean countries, to prepare the most flavorful fish stew, whole scaled fish is used. After cooking, the head and tail are removed and the fish is deboned. It is considered close to an art to nimbly and neatly bone fish using a knife and fork. However, a delicious stew can also be made without a whole fish —whatever seems more appealing to the cook.

CHAPTER SEVEN

Meats, Poultry and Game

*Cauliflower Gratin
(page 171), Hunter's Veal
Chops (page 145)
Above: Hilltop villa in
Tuscany*

COOKING ROASTS

Italians always allow their roasts to warm up to room temperature before cooking, a custom with which Americans may be uncomfortable due to concern about possible health hazards. Roasts at room temperature cook more uniformly, tend to shrink less and are more moist than roasts that are put into the oven very cold. One way to keep the roast tender without letting it warm to room temperature is to cut deep slits on all sides of the meat and insert bacon into the slits. The fat helps baste the meat as it cooks.

BEEF ROAST WITH PARMESAN AND CREAM

Manzo alla Panna

6 SERVINGS

2- to 3-pound beef rolled rump roast
½ teaspoon pepper
2 ounces Parmesan cheese, cut into 2 × ¼ × ¼-inch strips
2 tablespoons butter
2 tablespoons olive oil
½ cup dry red wine
2 cups whipping (heavy) cream
Salt and freshly ground pepper to taste
½ cup freshly grated Parmesan cheese

◆ Sprinkle beef roast with ½ teaspoon pepper. Make small, deep cuts in all sides of beef with sharp knife. Insert 1 cheese strip completely in each cut. Heat butter and oil in 4-quart Dutch oven over medium-high heat. Cook beef in butter mixture, turning occasionally, until brown. Add wine. Cook until wine is evaporated.

Pour ⅔ cup of the whipping cream over beef; reduce heat. Cover and simmer 2 hours, adding one-third of the remaining whipping cream at 20-minute intervals.

Sprinkle with salt and pepper. Place beef on warm platter; keep warm. Skim fat from juices in Dutch oven. Stir grated cheese into juices. Heat to boiling over medium heat, stirring constantly. Cut beef into thin slices; serve with sauce.

GRILLED MEATBALL KABOBS

Polpette allo Spiedo

4 SERVINGS

1 pound ground beef, pork and veal mixture
1 tablespoon chopped fresh parsley
1 tablespoon chopped fresh basil
1 teaspoon salt
1 teaspoon pepper
1 small onion, finely chopped (about ¼ cup)
2 cloves garlic, finely chopped
1 egg
1 large green bell pepper, cut into 1-inch squares

◆ Mix all ingredients except bell pepper. Shape mixture into 1-inch balls. Alternate meatballs and bell-pepper squares on each of four 12-inch metal skewers, leaving space between each meatball and bell-pepper square. Cover and grill kabobs about 4 inches from hot coals 10 minutes, turning frequently, until meat is done.

BROILED MEATBALL KABOBS: Set oven control to broil. Place kabobs on rack in broiler pan. Broil with tops about 3 inches from heat 5 minutes. Turn kabobs. Broil 4 to 5 minutes longer or until meat is done.

BRAISED BEEF TONGUE

Lingua in Salmi

4 SERVINGS

2-pound beef tongue
4 cups Chianti or dry red wine
1 tablespoon chopped fresh
    parsley
1 medium onion, chopped
    (about ½ cup)
1 medium carrot, chopped
    (about ½ cup)
2 cloves garlic, finely chopped
3 bay leaves
3 juniper berries
¼ cup olive oil
2 tablespoons butter
2 whole cloves
1 teaspoon salt
½ teaspoon pepper
3 tablespoons all-purpose flour
½ cup water

◆ Place tongue in large glass or plastic bowl. Mix wine, parsley, onion, carrot, garlic, bay leaves and juniper berries; pour over tongue. Cover tightly and refrigerate 12 hours.

Remove tongue from marinade; reserve marinade. Heat oil and butter in 4-quart Dutch oven over medium-high heat. Cook tongue in butter mixture, turning occasionally, until brown. Pour about half of the marinade (including the 3 bay leaves) over tongue; add cloves. Heat to boiling. Reduce heat to medium; cover and cook 1 hour.

Place remaining marinade in food processor or in blender; cover and process until smooth. Pour over tongue; sprinkle with salt and pepper. Cover and simmer 1 to 1½ hours or until tender.

Remove tongue from marinade; peel off skin. Cut tongue crosswise into ½-inch slices. Place on warm platter; keep warm.

Heat marinade to boiling. Boil uncovered until reduced to about 1¼ cups. Mix flour and water; stir into marinade. Heat to boiling, stirring constantly; boil and stir 1 minute. Strain marinade to remove whole spices. Pour marinade over tongue.

GRILLED FLORENTINE STEAKS

Bistecca alla Fiorentina   *4 SERVINGS*

1/4 cup chopped fresh parsley
1/4 cup olive oil
1 teaspoon salt
1 teaspoon pepper
4 cloves garlic, cut into pieces
4 beef T-bone steaks, about 1
   inch thick

◆ Place all ingredients except beef steaks in food processor or blender. Cover and process until smooth.

Cover and grill beef about 4 inches from hot coals 16 minutes, turning once and brushing with oil mixture frequently, until done.

BROILED FLORENTINE STEAKS: Set oven control to broil. Slash diagonally outer edge of fat on beef steaks at 1-inch intervals to prevent curling (do not cut into lean). Place beef on rack in broiler pan. Broil with tops 2 to 3 inches from heat 10 minutes, brushing with oil mixture frequently, until brown. Turn beef; broil 10 to 15 minutes, brushing with oil mixture frequently, until beef is done.

BRAISED VEAL ROAST

Vitello in Padella   *4 SERVINGS*

1/4 cup finely chopped prosciutto or fully cooked Virginia ham (about 2 ounces)
2 tablespoons chopped fresh
   sage
2 cloves garlic, finely chopped
2-pound veal boneless loin roast
3 tablespoons butter
1 small onion, thinly sliced
1/2 teaspoon salt
1/2 teaspoon pepper
1 cup Chianti or dry red wine
1 cup whipping (heavy) cream

◆ Mix prosciutto, sage and garlic. Make about 30 deep cuts in veal roast; place 1/2 teaspoon prosciutto mixture in each cut. Heat butter in 4-quart Dutch oven over medium heat. Sauté onion in butter. Reduce heat to low. Cook veal in onion mixture until brown. Sprinkle with salt and pepper. Add wine; cook uncovered over medium heat until liquid is reduced to about 1/3 cup. Add about half the whipping cream. Cover and simmer about 1 hour, adding remaining whipping cream gradually, about every 15 minutes, until veal is done.

VEAL WITH CAPER SAUCE
Vitello Tonnato ai Capperi

6 SERVINGS

½ teaspoon pepper
2-pound veal boneless loin roast
½ pound sliced bacon
I tablespoon olive oil
3 tablespoons olive oil
3 tablespoons lemon juice
I tablespoon capers, drained
I can (6½ ounces) tuna in oil,
  drained
4 flat fillets of anchovy
I hard-cooked egg yolk
Lemon wedges
Parsley sprigs

◆ Heat oven to 325°. Sprinkle pepper on veal roast. Wrap bacon slices around veal. Insert meat thermometer so tip is in center of thickest part of veal and does not rest in fat. Drizzle I tablespoon oil over bottom of shallow roasting pan. Place veal in pan. Roast uncovered I hour or until thermometer registers 170°. Let stand 15 minutes. Remove bacon and discard. Cut veal into thin slices; arrange on serving platter.

Place 3 tablespoons oil, the lemon juice, capers, tuna, fillets of anchovy and egg yolk in food processor or blender. Cover and process until light and foamy. Pour sauce over veal. Cover and refrigerate at least 12 hours but no longer than 24 hours. Serve cold with lemon wedges and parsley.

HUNTER'S VEAL CHOPS
Bistecchine alla Cacciatora

4 SERVINGS

¼ cup olive oil
I medium onion, thinly sliced
4 veal loin or rib chops, ½ inch
  thick
½ cup all-purpose flour
½ cup Chianti or dry red wine
½ teaspoon salt
½ teaspoon pepper
½ cup sliced fresh mushrooms
½ cup chicken broth
I can (28 ounces) imported
  pear-shaped tomatoes,
  drained and chopped

◆ Heat oil in 12-inch skillet over medium-high heat. Sauté onion in oil. Coat veal chops with flour. Cook veal in onion mixture over medium heat 8 minutes, turning once, until veal is brown.

Add wine; cook uncovered over medium-high heat until liquid is evaporated. Add salt, pepper, mushrooms, broth and tomatoes. Cook uncovered over medium-low heat 12 minutes or until veal is tender.

This hearty recipe is attributed to hunters who used basic ingredients—olive oil, tomatoes, mushrooms and wine—to flavor their catch. Whether wild rabbit or other game or veal from the market is used, a cacciatore combines meat and pantry basics into a memorable dish.

"JUMP-IN-THE-MOUTH" VEAL

Saltimbocca alla Romana

4 SERVINGS

The translation of this dish is "jump in the mouth," a whimsical description of how the combination of flavors springs to life when you bite into saltimbocca. Italians prefer veal to beef, especially milk-fed veal, and saltimbocca is delicious with either vitello, milk-fed veal, or vitellone, grass-fed veal. Vitellone is tougher, and needs to be pounded very thinly to ensure that the veal is tender.

8 small slices veal, ¼ inch thick (about 1½ pounds)
1 cup all-purpose flour
8 thin slices prosciutto or fully cooked Virginia ham
8 thin slices mozzarella cheese
8 fresh sage leaves
¼ cup butter
½ cup dry white wine
½ teaspoon salt
½ teaspoon pepper

◆ Pound each slice veal to tenderize. Coat with flour. Layer 1 slice each of prosciutto and cheese and 1 sage leaf on each piece of veal. Roll up; secure with wooden pick. Heat butter in 10-inch skillet over medium heat. Cook veal rolls in butter, turning occasionally, until brown. Add wine; sprinkle with salt and pepper. Cover and cook over medium-high heat 4 minutes.

SAUTÉED VEAL IN WINE SAUCE

Piccata di Vitello

4 SERVINGS

The term piccata is a variant on piccante, or spicy. Thinly sliced veal is wrapped in a wonderfully spicy, tangy sauce of wine and capers and should be served immediately from the skillet to the table.

8 small slices veal, ¼ inch thick (about 1½ pounds)
½ cup all-purpose flour
¼ cup butter
3 cloves garlic, finely chopped
1 tablespoon capers, drained
½ cup dry Marsala or dry red wine
½ teaspoon salt
½ teaspoon pepper

◆ Pound each veal slice to tenderize. Coat veal with flour. Heat butter in 10-inch skillet over medium-high heat. Sauté garlic in butter. Add veal, cook veal, turning once, until brown. Add capers and wine; sprinkle with salt and pepper. Cook uncovered over low heat until wine is evaporated. Place veal on warm platter; pour any remaining juices from skillet over veal.

"Jump-in-the-Mouth" Veal, Asparagus with Mushroom Sauce Flambé (page 168)

The Italian term soffritto is similar to the French term sauté, meaning to fry food quickly in butter or oil. However, it is more than just a way to cook; it is the base of most Italian sauce recipes, and is generally composed of garlic, tomatoes, onions, carrots, parsley and basil. The ingredients are cooked beyond the just-crisp stage to appassito, or "fading," the heat is lowered and cooking continues until all the ingredients are softened and blend together.

SPICED VEAL ROLLS

Involtini di Vitello Speziati

4 SERVINGS

2 tablespoons butter

2 tablespoons chopped onion

½ cup chopped carrots

1 clove garlic, finely chopped

½ pound mild bulk Italian sausage

½ teaspoon finely chopped fresh sage

½ teaspoon finely chopped fresh rosemary

½ teaspoon finely chopped fresh basil

1 tablespoon freshly grated Parmesan cheese

12 veal cutlets, 4 inches in diameter (about 2 pounds)

1 can (16 ounces) whole tomatoes, drained and chopped

2 tablespoons dry Marsala or dry red wine

½ teaspoon salt

½ teaspoon pepper

◆ Heat butter in 10-inch skillet over medium-high heat. Sauté onion, carrots and garlic in butter. Add sausage; cook uncovered over medium heat 10 minutes, stirring frequently; drain and reserve juices.

Mix sausage mixture, sage, rosemary, basil and cheese. Spoon 1 rounded tablespoon of the sausage mixture on center of each veal cutlet and roll up. Secure with wooden pick. Pour reserved juices into skillet. Add veal rolls. Cook uncovered over medium heat 5 minutes, turning occasionally, until brown. Add tomatoes, wine, salt and pepper. Heat to boiling; reduce heat. Cover and simmer 20 minutes.

VEAL MILAN-STYLE

Fettine alla Milanese

6 SERVINGS

6 veal or beef cutlets, ½ inch
    thick
Salt
Freshly ground pepper
2 eggs, beaten
1 tablespoon lemon juice
¼ cup all-purpose flour
1 cup Italian-style dry bread
    crumbs
½ cup butter
Parsley sprigs
1 lemon, cut into wedges

◆ Flatten each veal cutlet to ¼-inch thickness between plastic wrap or waxed paper. Sprinkle with salt and pepper. Mix eggs and lemon juice. Coat veal with flour. Dip veal into egg mixture; coat with bread crumbs. Heat butter in 12-inch skillet over medium heat. Cook veal in butter 8 minutes, turning once, until veal is light golden brown. Place veal on warm platter; pour any remaining juices from skillet over veal. Garnish with parsley and lemon.

STUFFED PUMPKIN

Zucca Ripiena

4 TO 6 SERVINGS

5-pound pumpkin
1½ cups Sugo Sauce (page 84)
¼ cup butter
2 medium baking potatoes,
    pared and chopped (about
    2 cups)
2 medium stalks celery, chopped
    (about 1 cup)
2 medium carrots, chopped
    (about 1 cup)
1 medium onion, chopped (about
    ½ cup)
1 pound veal stew meat
½ cup prosciutto or fully cooked
    Virginia ham, chopped
    (about 3 ounces)
1 cup dry white wine
1 teaspoon ground cloves
1 cup shredded mozzarella
    cheese (4 ounces)

◆ Heat oven to 350°. Remove pumpkin stem if necessary. Cut pumpkin crosswise in half; remove strings and seeds. Place cut sides down on ungreased cookie sheet. Bake about 1 hour or until tender.

Prepare Sugo Sauce. Heat butter in 12-inch skillet over medium-high heat. Sauté potatoes, celery, carrots and onion in butter. Stir in veal and prosciutto. Cook uncovered about 10 minutes, stirring frequently, until veal is brown. Stir in wine. Heat to boiling; reduce heat. Simmer uncovered until liquid is evaporated. Stir in Sugo Sauce and cloves. Heat to boiling; reduce heat. Cover and simmer about 20 minutes or until veal is done.

Spoon veal mixture into pumpkin halves; top with cheese. Bake uncovered 8 to 10 minutes or until cheese is melted. Cut in wedges to serve.

PORK ROAST WITH ROSEMARY

Arista Arrosto al Rosmarino

6 TO 8 SERVINGS

2½- to 3-pound pork loin roast
2 tablespoons fresh rosemary
4 cloves garlic
1 teaspoon salt
1 teaspoon pepper
2 tablespoons butter
1 small onion, chopped (about
    ¼ cup)
¼ cup olive oil

◆ Heat oven to 350°. Trim fat from pork roast. Finely chop rosemary and garlic together. Make 8 to 10 deep cuts, about 2 inches apart, in pork with sharp knife. Insert small amounts of garlic mixture in cuts. Sprinkle with salt and pepper.

Heat butter in shallow roasting pan in oven; sprinkle with onion. Place pork in pan; drizzle with oil. Insert meat thermometer so tip is in center of thickest part of pork and does not rest in fat. Roast uncovered 1¾ to 2 hours or until thermometer registers 170°. Let stand 15 minutes before slicing.

PEPPERED PORK CHOPS

Costolette di Maiale al Pepe

4 SERVINGS

1 tablespoon whole black pep-
    percorns, coarsely crushed
6 pork loin chops, ½ inch thick
¼ cup butter
2 tablespoons olive oil
4 cloves garlic, cut in half
1 cup sliced fresh mushrooms
½ teaspoon salt
½ cup Marsala or dry red wine

◆ Sprinkle half of the crushed peppercorns over one side of pork chops; gently press into pork. Turn pork and repeat with remaining peppercorns.

Heat butter and oil in 12-inch skillet over medium-high heat. Sauté garlic until golden. Add pork; cook uncovered 5 minutes. Turn pork; add mushrooms, salt and wine. Cover and simmer about 5 minutes longer or until pork is done.

Pork Roast with Rosemary

**Olive trees,
Populonia, Tuscany**

FILLED PORK CHOPS

Involtini di Maiale

4 SERVINGS

4 pork loin chops, 1 inch thick
¼ cup Italian-style dry bread
    crumbs
1 tablespoon plus 1 teaspoon
    freshly grated Parmesan
    cheese
1 tablespoon plus 1 teaspoon
    finely chopped prosciutto
    or fully cooked Virginia ham
1 green onion (with top),
    chopped
1 egg
¼ cup butter
1 green onion (with top),
    chopped
1 green bell pepper, cut into
    strips
½ teaspoon salt
½ teaspoon pepper
1 cup Marsala or dry red wine

◆ Make a cut in each pork chop to form a pocket. Mix bread crumbs, cheese, prosciutto, 1 onion and the egg. Fill pockets with bread mixture. Heat butter in 12-inch skillet over medium-high heat. Sauté 1 onion and the bell pepper in butter.

Add pork and cook uncovered over medium heat, turning once, until brown. Sprinkle with salt and pepper; add wine. Heat to boiling; reduce heat. Cover and cook over low heat 45 minutes or until pork is done.

SPRING LAMB

Agnello di Primavera

4 SERVINGS

2 tablespoons butter

1 medium onion, finely chopped
(about ½ cup)

2 cloves garlic, finely chopped

8 lean lamb loin chops, ½ inch
thick (about 1½ pounds)

¼ cup all-purpose flour

1 cup dry white wine

2 tablespoons brandy

1 cup whipping (heavy) cream

2 tablespoons lemon juice

½ teaspoon salt

½ teaspoon freshly grated
nutmeg

½ teaspoon pepper

◆ Heat butter in 12-inch skillet over medium-high heat. Sauté onion and garlic in butter. Coat lamb chops with flour. Cook lamb in onion mixture, turning once, until brown. Pour wine and brandy over lamb. Cook uncovered until liquid is evaporated.

Add remaining ingredients. Heat to boiling; reduce heat to low. Cover and cook over low heat about 30 minutes, stirring occasionally, until lamb is tender.

GRILLED LAMB CHOPS WITH MINT

Costolette d'Agnello alla Menta

4 SERVINGS

8 lamb loin chops, ½ inch thick

½ cup chopped fresh mint

½ cup wine vinegar

½ cup olive oil

1 tablespoon sugar

½ teaspoon salt

½ teaspoon pepper

◆ Place lamb chops in rectangular baking dish, 11 × 7 × 1½ inches. Place ¼ cup of the mint and the remaining ingredients in food processor or blender. Cover and process until smooth. Pour over lamb. Cover and refrigerate 1 hour.

Remove lamb from marinade; reserve marinade. Toss remaining mint onto hot coals. Cover and grill lamb about 4 inches from coals 10 minutes, turning once and brushing with marinade occasionally, until lamb is done.

BROILED LAMB CHOPS WITH MINT: Omit ¼ cup chopped fresh mint. Set oven control to broil. Place marinaded lamb chops on rack in broiler pan. Broil with tops about 2 inches from heat about 6 minutes or until brown. Turn lamb. Broil 5 to 6 minutes longer or until lamb is done.

LAMB

In the Mediterranean countries lamb is a favorite dish. It is a particular favorite in the south of Italy as its drier climate is more conducive to raising sheep and goats than to the production of beef and pork common in northern Italy. Sardinia is foremost in sheep raising, and throughout southern Italy ewe's milk is prized to make flavorful Romano cheese. Spring lamb is a particular treat, whether served at Easter or any other time in the spring while lambs are still milk fed.

GRILLED MEAT AND VEGETABLE KABOBS

Spiedini Fantasia

4 TO 6 SERVINGS

1 pound lamb boneless shoulder, cut into 1-inch cubes
1 pound veal or beef tenderloin,
  cut into 1-inch cubes
½ cup Basil-Garlic Sauce (page
  85)
½ cup dry white wine
3 tablespoons lemon juice
8 ounces fresh medium mushrooms, stems removed
1 red bell pepper, cut into
  1-inch pieces
1 green bell pepper, cut into
  1-inch pieces
1 yellow bell pepper, cut into
  1-inch pieces
16 fresh bay or sage leaves
2 leeks, cut into 1-inch pieces
8 cherry tomatoes

◆ Place lamb and veal in glass or plastic bowl. Mix Basil-Garlic Sauce, wine and lemon juice; pour over meat. Cover and refrigerate 1 hour.

Remove meat from marinade; reserve marinade. Alternate meat, mushrooms, bell peppers, bay leaves and leeks on each of eight 9-inch metal skewers, leaving space between each piece of food. Top each skewer with tomato.

Cover and grill kabobs about 4 inches from hot coals 16 minutes, turning once and brushing with marinade occasionally, until meat is done.

BROILED MEAT AND VEGETABLE KABOBS: Set oven control to broil. Place kabobs on rack in broiler pan. Broil with tops about 3 inches from heat 5 minutes. Turn kabobs; brush with marinade. Broil 5 minutes. Turn kabobs; brush with marinade. Broil 5 minutes longer or until meat is done.

*Grilled Meat-and-
Vegetable Kabobs*

Tuscan countryside

GRILLED LAMB AND SAUSAGE KABOBS

Spiedini d'Agnello e Salsiccia　　　　　　　　*6 SERVINGS*

1 pound lamb boneless shoulder, cut into 1-inch cubes
1/2 cup olive oil
3 tablespoons lemon juice
1 tablespoon chopped fresh parsley
1 tablespoon chopped fresh sage
1/2 teaspoon salt
1/2 teaspoon pepper
1 clove garlic
1 pound sweet Italian sausage links
18 fresh or dried bay leaves
18 fresh mushroom caps

◆ Place lamb in glass or plastic bowl. Place oil, lemon juice, parsley, sage, salt, pepper and garlic in food processor or blender. Cover and process until smooth. Pour over lamb. Cover and refrigerate 30 minutes.

Remove lamb from marinade; reserve marinade. Cut sausage into eighteen 1-inch pieces. Alternate lamb, sausage, bay leaves and mushroom caps on each of six 10-inch metal skewers, leaving space between each piece of food. Cover and grill kabobs about 4 inches from hot coals 10 minutes, turning kabobs and brushing with marinade occasionally, until meat is done.

BROILED LAMB AND SAUSAGE KABOBS: Set oven control to broil. Place kabobs on rack in broiler pan. Broil with tops about 3 inches from heat 5 minutes. Turn kabobs; brush with marinade. Broil 5 minutes. Turn kabobs; brush with marinade. Broil 5 minutes longer or until meat is done.

MUTTON WITH SPICY SAUCE

Montone Piccante

6 SERVINGS

½ cup olive oil

1 tablespoon capers, drained

2 pounds boneless mutton or
    lamb, cut into 1-inch pieces

1 medium onion, thinly sliced

1 cup Sugo Sauce (page 84)

½ cup dry white wine

1 tablespoon chopped fresh
    parsley

½ teaspoon salt

½ teaspoon pepper

2 green bell peppers, cut into
    ½-inch strips

1 small red chili, seeded and
    finely chopped

◆ Heat oil in 12-inch skillet until hot. Cook capers, mutton and onion in oil, stirring occasionally, until mutton is brown. Stir in remaining ingredients. Heat to boiling; reduce heat. Cover and simmer 1 hour, stirring occasionally, until mutton is tender.

BRANDIED CHICKEN

Pollo al Brandy

6 SERVINGS

¼ cup butter

3- to 3½-pound broiler-fryer
    chicken, cut up

1 medium onion, thinly sliced

½ teaspoon salt

½ teaspoon pepper

2 tablespoons chopped fresh
    parsley

1 cup Italian brandy

2 cups sliced fresh mushrooms

¾ cup whipping (heavy) cream

1 tablespoon all-purpose flour

1 egg yolk, slightly beaten

◆ Heat butter in 10-inch skillet over medium-high heat. Cook chicken and onion in butter, turning occasionally, until chicken is brown. Sprinkle with salt, pepper and parsley. Add brandy; reduce heat to low. Cover and cook 30 minutes. Add mushrooms; cover and cook 15 minutes longer or until juices from chicken run clear. Remove from heat.

Beat whipping cream, flour and egg yolk in 1-quart saucepan until smooth. Heat to boiling, stirring constantly. Cook and stir 1 minute. Pour over chicken to form a glaze.

CHICKEN BREASTS IN LEMON-CAPER SAUCE

Piccata di Pollo

4 SERVINGS

4 skinless, boneless chicken
   breast halves (about 1½
   pounds)
½ cup all-purpose flour
¼ cup butter
2 teaspoons chopped garlic
1 cup dry white wine
2 tablespoons lemon juice
½ teaspoon pepper
1 tablespoon large capers,
   drained
Strawberries
Parsley sprigs

◆ Cut each chicken breast horizontally to make 2 thin slices. Coat with flour. Heat butter in 12-inch skillet over medium-high heat. Cook chicken and garlic in butter 4 to 6 minutes, turning once, until chicken is brown. Add wine and lemon juice; sprinkle with pepper. Heat until hot. Sprinkle with capers. Garnish with strawberries and parsley.

FLAMBÉED CHICKEN

Pollo alla Fiamma

4 SERVINGS

2½- to 3-pound broiler-fryer
   chicken, cut lengthwise in
   half
1 teaspoon salt
½ teaspoon pepper
18 sprigs fresh rosemary
3 cloves garlic, cut in half
3 tablespoons butter
½ cup light rum

◆ Rub chicken with salt and pepper. Place 3 sprigs rosemary in 3 different areas under skin of each half chicken. Cook chicken and garlic in butter in 12-inch skillet over medium-high heat, turning occasionally, until chicken is brown. Cover and cook over medium heat 40 minutes or until chicken juices run clear. Pour rum into skillet. Heat about 1 minute or until hot. Carefully ignite. Serve when flame dies out.

Since Roman times, capers have been a basic ingredient in Italy's favorite sauces. Caper bushes grow throughout the Mediterranean countries; caper buds are picked and pickled before they flower.

Some dishes are flamed only for dramatic effect, but flaming can also be an important part of the cooking process. The alcohol is burned off, but the flavor of the rum remains. Use the amount of rum that is called for—too much alcohol and the flames can burn the chicken, leaving a charred taste. Flames should not burn longer than a minute and, as a safety precaution, a lid should always be on hand to extinguish the flames, if necessary. Normally, rum, vodka and other spirits will burn themselves out in a minute, but they can flame up if the dish is placed over heat again.

**Chicken Breasts in
Lemon-Caper Sauce**

ANISETTE CHICKEN BREASTS

Petti di Pollo al Sambuca

4 SERVINGS

4 skinless, boneless chicken
    breast halves (about 1½
    pounds)
2 tablespoons butter
2 tablespoons olive oil
1 teaspoon salt
½ teaspoon pepper
2 cups sliced fresh mushrooms
¼ cup milk
2 tablespoons all-purpose flour
2 tablespoons whipping (heavy)
    cream
¼ cup licorice-flavored liqueur

◆ Flatten each chicken breast half to ¼-inch thickness between plastic wrap. Heat butter and oil in 12-inch skillet over medium-high heat. Cook chicken in butter mixture, turning occasionally, until brown. Sprinkle with salt and pepper. Add mushrooms. Cover and cook over medium heat 15 minutes. Remove chicken and mushrooms with slotted spoon onto warm platter and keep warm.

Mix milk, flour and whipping cream until smooth. Heat liquid in skillet to boiling; gradually stir in milk mixture. Add liqueur; heat to boiling, stirring constantly. Boil and stir 4 minutes. Pour sauce over chicken.

CHICKEN LIVERS WITH MARSALA SAUCE

Fegatini di Pollo al Marsala

4 SERVINGS

1 pound chicken livers
2 small onions
2 cloves garlic
2 tablespoons butter
1 tablespoon chopped fresh
  sage
1 teaspoon salt
1 teaspoon pepper
1 tablespoon all-purpose flour
1 cup dry Marsala or dry red
  wine

◆ Wash chicken livers; pat dry. Cut livers in half.

Place onions and garlic in food processor or blender. Cover and process until finely chopped, stirring occasionally.

Cook onion mixture in butter in 10-inch skillet over low heat 8 minutes. Stir in livers, sage, salt and pepper. Cook over medium-high heat 8 minutes, stirring frequently. Place liver mixture on warm platter; keep warm.

Stir flour into skillet. Heat over medium heat, stirring constantly, until bubbly. Remove from heat. Gradually stir in wine. Heat to boiling, stirring constantly; boil and stir 1 minute. Spoon sauce over livers.

TURKEY WITH BRANDIED CHEESE SAUCE

Tacchino al Latte

4 SERVINGS

4 slices uncooked turkey breast, ½ inch thick (about 1½ pounds)

2 cups milk

½ teaspoon salt

¼ teaspoon pepper

½ cup all-purpose flour

¼ cup butter

¼ cup Italian brandy

4 thin slices Fontina cheese

◆ Flatten turkey to ¼-inch thickness between plastic wrap or waxed paper. Pour milk over turkey; cover and refrigerate 1½ hours.

Drain turkey; sprinkle with salt and pepper. Coat turkey with flour. Heat butter in 12-inch skillet over medium heat. Add turkey; cover and cook 8 minutes. Add brandy; cook uncovered until liquid is evaporated. Turn turkey; top with cheese. Cover and cook about 5 minutes or until cheese is melted.

WILD TURKEY WITH ORANGE SAUCE

Tacchino Selvatico all'Arancia

6 SERVINGS

2 pounds boneless wild or domestic turkey, cut into 1-inch cubes

1 large onion, sliced

2 tablespoons chopped fresh parsley

½ cup dry white wine

⅓ cup orange juice

¼ cup butter

1 teaspoon salt

1 teaspoon pepper

2 heads romaine, chopped

¼ cup orange-flavored liqueur

1 orange

◆ Place turkey, onion and parsley in glass or plastic bowl. Pour wine and orange juice over top. Cover and refrigerate 1 hour, stirring occasionally.

Remove turkey from marinade; pat dry. Remove onion from marinade with slotted spoon; reserve marinade. Heat butter in 12-inch skillet over medium-high heat. Sauté onion in butter. Stir in turkey. Cook, stirring occasionally, until turkey is brown. Sprinkle with salt and pepper; cover with romaine. Pour marinade over romaine. Cover and cook over medium heat 1 hour. Stir in liqueur; simmer uncovered 5 minutes.

Pare orange; cut into slices. Cut each slice into fourths. Carefully stir orange into turkey mixture.

Turkeys came to Europe in the sixteenth century from the New World, part of the culinary bounty brought back by explorers. Turkey was first documented as being eaten in Italy in 1570 at the wedding of the Florentine Duchess Isabella de Medici and King Charles IX of France. In her honor, whole turkeys were cooked in giant fireplaces, then carefully and laboriously redressed in their plumage, forming the centerpiece at the wedding feast.

STUFFED QUAIL
Quaglie Ripiene

4 SERVINGS

1/4 cup water

2 tablespoons chopped fresh
  parsley

2 tablespoons pine nuts

1/2 teaspoon salt

1/2 teaspoon pepper

4 slices Italian bread, 1/2 inch
  thick, torn into small pieces

4 thin slices prosciutto or fully
  cooked Virginia ham

4 cloves garlic, finely chopped

1 hard-cooked egg, chopped

4 quail (6 to 8 ounces each)

8 slices bacon

3 tablespoons olive oil

◆ Heat oven to 375°. Mix all ingredients except quail, bacon and oil. Fill each quail with bread mixture. Wrap 2 slices bacon around each quail; secure with wooden picks. Place breast sides up at least 1 inch apart in shallow roasting pan. Drizzle oil over quail. Roast uncovered 1 hour or until done.

PHEASANT STEW
Fagiano in Tegame

4 SERVINGS

2 tablespoons butter

1/2 cup chopped lean bacon

1 medium onion, thinly sliced

1 pheasant, cut into fourths

1/2 cup dry white wine

1/2 teaspoon salt

1/2 teaspoon pepper

1/2 cup chicken broth

2 tablespoons chopped fresh
  sage

2 tablespoons chopped fresh
  rosemary

2 medium carrots, thinly sliced

◆ Heat butter in 12-inch skillet over medium-high heat. Cook bacon and onion in butter until bacon is crisp. Cook pheasant in bacon mixture over medium-high heat, turning occasionally, until pheasant is brown. Add wine. Cook uncovered until liquid is evaporated. Sprinkle with salt and pepper. Add remaining ingredients. Cover and cook over medium heat 1 hour.

HUNTER'S RABBIT
Coniglio alla Cacciatora

6 SERVINGS

1/2 cup olive oil
1 medium onion, sliced
2 1/2- to 3-pound rabbit, cut into
    2-inch pieces
1/2 cup all-purpose flour
1/2 teaspoon salt
1/2 teaspoon pepper
1 cup dry white wine
2 cups sliced fresh mushrooms
1 cup imported Italian black
    olives, pitted
1 cup canned imported pear-
    shaped tomatoes, drained
    and chopped
1/2 cup chicken broth

◆ Heat oil in 12-inch skillet over medium-high heat. Sauté onion in oil. Coat rabbit with flour. Cook rabbit in onion mixture over medium heat, turning occasionally, until brown. Sprinkle with salt and pepper. Stir in wine. Cook uncovered until liquid is evaporated. Stir in remaining ingredients. Cover and simmer 1 hour.

Italians frequently cook and serve rabbit whole as they do chicken, including the head, feet and bones. They check to see if the meat is done by how easily the meat pulls away from the bone, and the skill with which one removes bones is an essential part of good table manners.

VENISON WITH ROSEMARY SAUCE
Cervo al Rosmarino

4 SERVINGS

8 venison chops or steaks, 1/2
    inch thick
1/2 teaspoon salt
1/2 teaspoon pepper
1/4 cup butter
1 tablespoon chopped fresh
    rosemary
2 cloves garlic, cut in half
1/4 cup Chianti or dry red wine
1/4 cup whipping (heavy) cream

◆ Trim fat from venison chops. Sprinkle venison with salt and pepper. Heat butter in 12-inch skillet. Cook rosemary and garlic in butter over medium heat until garlic is golden. Add venison. Cook uncovered 10 minutes, turning once, until venison is brown. Add wine and whipping cream. Cover and cook over low heat 10 minutes or until venison is tender.

Venison with Rosemary Sauce, Fresh Peas and Prosciutto (page 174)

CHAPTER EIGHT

Taste from the Garden

Wild Mushroom Pie (page 175), Tomato and Potato Salad with Herbs (page 185)
Above: Detail of a balustrade and grape arbor, Sovrano, Lazio

Italians love both carciofi (artichokes) and the spiny cardi (the leaves from a Mediterranean plant closely related to the artichoke). Artichokes are marinated in olive oil and spices, eaten raw with salt and pepper or cooked in casseroles as they are here. Cardoons, as cardi are known in English, have a slightly bitter taste, so when they are cleaned and their spiny edges removed, they are best deep fried or cooked in a tomato sauce with cheese.

ARTICHOKE HEARTS WITH OLIVES AND POTATOES

Carciofi Rustici

4 SERVINGS

2 packages (9 ounces each) frozen artichoke hearts
2 tablespoons lemon juice
1 pound small red potatoes, cut in halves
2 cups Chicken Broth (page 17)
½ cup olive oil
1 small onion, thinly sliced
1 cup sliced pitted green olives
1 teaspoon capers, drained
½ teaspoon salt
¼ teaspoon pepper
Freshly grated Parmesan cheese

◆ Place frozen artichoke hearts in large bowl; add lemon juice and enough water to cover. Let stand until artichoke hearts are thawed; drain. Place potatoes in 3-quart saucepan; add Chicken Broth and enough water to cover. Heat to boiling; reduce heat. Cover and simmer about 10 minutes or until tender; drain.

Heat oil in 12-inch skillet over medium-high heat. Sauté onion in oil. Reduce heat to medium; stir in artichoke hearts, potatoes and remaining ingredients except cheese. Cook uncovered about 5 minutes, stirring frequently, until hot. Sprinkle with cheese.

ASPARAGUS WITH MUSHROOM SAUCE FLAMBÉ

Asparagi con Funghi alla Fiamma

4 SERVINGS

1 quart water
1 teaspoon salt
1 pound fresh asparagus spears
¼ cup butter
2 tablespoons chopped fresh parsley
2 cloves garlic, finely chopped
2 cups sliced fresh mushrooms
½ cup brandy
2 tablespoons lemon juice

◆ Heat water and salt to boiling. Add asparagus spears. Heat to boiling; boil uncovered 5 minutes. Cover and boil about 7 minutes or until stalks are tender; drain.

Heat butter in 10-inch skillet over medium-high heat. Sauté parsley and garlic in butter. Reduce heat to medium; stir in mushrooms. Cook uncovered about 6 minutes, stirring frequently, until mushrooms are tender. Place asparagus on mushrooms; pour brandy over asparagus. Heat over high heat until brandy is hot; carefully ignite. Pour lemon juice over asparagus and mushroom mixture when flame dies out.

Artichoke Hearts with Olives and Potatoes

GREEN BEANS WITH LEMON BUTTER

Fagiolini al Limone   *4 SERVINGS*

2 cups Chicken Broth (page
  17)
2 cups water
1 pound fresh green beans
¼ cup butter
1 small onion, thinly sliced
3 tablespoons lemon juice
1 egg, beaten
1 tablespoon chopped fresh
  parsley

◆ Heat Chicken Broth and water to boiling. Add green beans. Cover and boil about 8 minutes or until tender; drain. Heat butter in 10-inch skillet over medium-high heat. Sauté onion in butter. Add beans and lemon juice; stir in egg. Cook 3 minutes, stirring frequently, until egg is cooked. Sprinkle with parsley.

BOK CHOY WITH CREAM SAUCE

Barbabietole alla Crema   *4 SERVINGS*

Bok choy is a staple in the Italian Riviera, boiled either alone or with other vegetables, and then topped with a cream sauce. In Genoa, bok choy is used to make a special Easter cake. A bok-choy-and-egg mixture is placed between layers of puff pastry for an unusual treat.

1 pound bok choy
2 tablespoons butter
1 cup whipping (heavy) cream
2 tablespoons lemon juice
½ teaspoon salt
½ teaspoon dry mustard
¼ teaspoon pepper
2 green onions (with tops),
  thinly sliced

◆ Cut bok choy leaves from stems; cut leaves in half. Cut stems lengthwise in half. Place steamer basket in ½ inch water (water should not touch bottom of basket). Place leaves and stems in basket. Cover tightly and heat to boiling; reduce heat. Steam 5 to 7 minutes or until stems are tender.

Heat butter in 1-quart saucepan over low heat. Stir in remaining ingredients. Heat to boiling; reduce heat. Simmer uncovered 5 minutes, stirring occasionally. Pour over bok choy.

BRUSSELS SPROUTS WITH PROSCIUTTO

Cavolini di Bruxelles al Prosciutto

4 SERVINGS

1 pound fresh Brussels sprouts
2 cups Chicken Broth (page 17)
¼ cup butter
1 small onion, thinly sliced
4 thin slices prosciutto or fully cooked Virginia ham, chopped
Freshly grated Parmesan cheese

◆ Place Brussels sprouts in 3-quart saucepan; add Chicken Broth and enough water to cover. Heat to boiling; reduce heat. Cover and simmer about 10 minutes or until tender; drain.

Heat butter in 10-inch skillet over medium-high heat. Sauté onion in butter. Stir in Brussels sprouts and prosciutto; reduce heat. Cover and simmer about 2 minutes or until hot. Sprinkle with cheese.

CAULIFLOWER GRATIN

Cavolfiore Gratinato

8 SERVINGS

2 medium heads cauliflower (about 2 pounds each), separated into 1-inch flowerets
1 small onion, sliced
1 cup diced prosciutto or fully cooked Virginia ham (about 8 ounces)
2 tablespoons butter
1 cup milk
½ cup whipping (heavy) cream
½ teaspoon salt
½ teaspoon white pepper
1 cup shredded Fontina cheese (4 ounces)
½ cup freshly grated Parmesan cheese
1 teaspoon freshly grated nutmeg

◆ Heat cauliflower and enough water to cover to boiling. Cover and boil 10 minutes; drain.

Heat oven to 375°. Cook onion and prosciutto in butter in 3-quart saucepan over low heat about 10 minutes, stirring occasionally, until onion is tender. Stir in milk and whipping cream. Heat to boiling; reduce heat. Simmer uncovered 10 minutes, stirring occasionally. Stir in cauliflower; pour into ungreased 3-quart casserole. Sprinkle with remaining ingredients. Bake uncovered about 20 minutes or until hot and bubbly.

CARROTS WITH RUM RAISINS

Carote al Rum

4 SERVINGS

½ cup light rum
½ cup raisins
6 pearl onions, peeled and cut
    in half
¼ cup butter
1½ pounds small whole carrots
½ cup dry white wine
1 teaspoon finely chopped fresh
    dill weed
½ teaspoon salt
½ teaspoon crushed red pepper
    flakes
1 cup whipping (heavy) cream

◆ Pour rum over raisins. Let stand 30 minutes.

Cook onions and butter in 10-inch skillet over low heat 5 minutes, stirring occasionally until onions begin to soften. Stir in carrots, raisins and rum. Cook until rum is evaporated. Stir in wine, dill weed, salt and red pepper flakes. Cover and cook over medium heat 20 minutes or until carrots are tender. Stir in whipping cream. Heat to boiling; boil uncovered 5 minutes.

CARROT PUDDING

Budino di Carote

8 SERVINGS

2 quarts water
1 tablespoon salt
2 pounds medium carrots, pared
    and cut crosswise in half
1 medium baking potato (about
    6 ounces), pared and cut
    into fourths
1 cup mayonnaise or salad
    dressing
½ cup chopped imported Italian
    black olives, pitted
½ cup chopped pitted green
    olives
1 tablespoon chopped fresh
    parsley
1 teaspoon chopped fresh dill
    weed
1 small onion, chopped (about
    ¼ cup)

◆ Heat water and salt to boiling. Add carrots and potato. Boil uncovered 18 to 20 minutes or until tender; drain and cool.

Place carrots and potato in food processor or blender; cover and process until smooth. Mix carrot mixture and remaining ingredients; cover and refrigerate 2 hours or until chilled.

Carrots with Rum Raisins

FRESH PEAS AND PROSCIUTTO

Piselli al Prosciutto per Contorno

4 SERVINGS

¼ cup olive oil

⅓ pound prosciutto or fully cooked
    Virginia ham, chopped

1 small onion, chopped (about
    ¼ cup)

2 pounds fresh green peas,
    shelled*

½ cup Chicken Broth (page
    17)

1 tablespoon sugar

1 tablespoon chopped fresh
    parsley

¼ teaspoon salt

◆ Heat oil in 10-inch skillet over medium-high heat. Sauté prosciutto and onion in oil. Reduce heat to medium; stir in remaining ingredients. Cover and cook about 10 minutes or until peas are tender.

*2½ cups frozen green peas can be substituted for the fresh green peas.

PEAS AND BASIL OMELET

Frittata al Basilico e Piselli

4 SERVINGS

The traditional way to cook a frittata is to invert the egg mixture onto a plate and then slide it back into the skillet. However, for some of us, it might be easier to finish cooking the frittata under the broiler. Broil the frittata with the top about 5 inches from the heat for 3 to 4 minutes or until golden brown. It will look and taste just as wonderful but be a little easier to handle.

5 jumbo eggs

⅓ cup chopped fresh basil

¼ cup whipping (heavy) cream

2 tablespoons freshly grated
    Parmesan cheese

½ teaspoon salt

¼ teaspoon pepper

1 cup fresh or frozen (thawed)
    green peas

¼ cup butter

1 small onion, finely chopped
    (about ¼ cup)

◆ Beat eggs, basil, whipping cream, cheese, salt and pepper; stir in peas. Heat butter in 10-inch nonstick skillet over medium-high heat. Sauté onion in butter.

Reduce heat to medium-low. Pour egg mixture into skillet. Cook uncovered, gently lifting edge so uncooked portion can flow to bottom, until eggs are almost set and golden brown on bottom. Place 10-inch plate or larger over skillet; invert omelet onto plate. Slide omelet back into skillet. Cook until eggs are set and golden brown on bottom.

WILD MUSHROOM PIE

Crostata di Funghi

6 TO 8 SERVINGS

2 cups all-purpose flour
¾ cup butter, softened
1 jumbo egg
2 tablespoons butter
1 small onion, thinly sliced
2 cups sliced fresh mushrooms
2 cups sliced porcini mushrooms
1 cup whole morel mushrooms
½ cup Marsala or dry red wine
1¼ cups whipping (heavy)
    cream
½ teaspoon salt
¼ teaspoon pepper
1½ cups ricotta cheese
1 cup shredded Fontina cheese
    (4 ounces)
½ cup freshly grated Parmesan
    cheese

◆ Mix flour, ¾ cup butter and the egg in large bowl until dough forms. Turn dough onto lightly floured surface. Knead lightly 1 or 2 minutes or until smooth. Cover and refrigerate 30 minutes.

Heat 2 tablespoons butter in 10-inch skillet over medium-high heat. Sauté onion in butter. Reduce heat to medium; stir in mushrooms. Cook uncovered 5 minutes. Stir in wine; cook until wine is evaporated. Stir in whipping cream; sprinkle with salt and pepper. Heat to boiling over medium heat; reduce heat. Cover and simmer 10 minutes; cool.

Move oven rack to lowest position. Heat oven to 350°. Roll dough into 14-inch circle. Ease dough into pie plate, 10 × 1½ inches, pressing firmly against bottom and side.

Mix mushroom mixture and cheeses. Spoon into pie plate; spread to make even. Trim excess dough from edge of plate. Bake 35 to 40 minutes or until set and crust is golden brown. Cool 10 to 15 minutes before cutting.

Hadrian's villa,
near Tivoli

ONION SOUFFLÉ WITH ASPARAGUS

Suffle di Cipolle e Asparagi   *4 SERVINGS*

½ cup olive oil
2 tablespoons butter
I pound pearl onions, peeled
   and cut in half
I package (10 ounces) frozen
   asparagus spears*
½ cup all-purpose flour
2 flat fillets of anchovy in oil,
   drained
½ cup freshly grated Parmesan
   cheese
I tablespoon chopped fresh
   tarragon
I teaspoon freshly grated
   nutmeg
I teaspoon salt
½ teaspoon pepper
4 eggs, separated

◆ Heat oven to 375°. Butter 6-cup soufflé dish. Heat oil and butter in 10-inch skillet over medium-high heat. Sauté onions in oil mixture, gently mashing, until soft; cool.

Cook asparagus as directed on package; drain well. Sprinkle flour over asparagus; toss until coated. Remove asparagus from flour, shaking off excess.

Place asparagus, onions and fillets of anchovy in food processor or in blender; cover and process until smooth. Mix asparagus mixture and remaining ingredients except egg whites thoroughly.

Beat egg whites in large bowl on high speed until stiff but not dry. Fold asparagus mixture into egg whites. Carefully pour into soufflé dish. Bake uncovered 30 to 40 minutes or until knife inserted halfway between center and edge comes out clean.

*1½ pounds cooked fresh asparagus spears can be substituted for the frozen asparagus spears.

STEWED GARBANZO BEANS WITH ONIONS

Fagioli in Umido con Cipolle

6 SERVINGS

1 pound dried garbanzo beans
  (about 2⅓ cups)
8 slices bacon, cut into ½-inch
  pieces
6 pearl onions, peeled and cut
  in half
3 tablespoons butter
2 cups Chicken Broth (page
  17)
½ teaspoon chopped fresh dill
  weed
½ teaspoon chopped fresh
  parsley
½ teaspoon pepper

◆ Pour enough water over garbanzo beans to cover 2 inches above beans. Let stand at least 8 hours; drain.

Cook bacon and onions in butter in 10-inch skillet over medium heat, stirring frequently, until bacon is crisp. Stir in beans and remaining ingredients. Heat to boiling; reduce heat. Cover and simmer 30 minutes or until beans are tender.

SPINACH, MILAN-STYLE

Spinaci alla Milanese

4 SERVINGS

2 pounds fresh spinach
2 tablespoons water
3 tablespoons butter
2 cloves garlic, finely chopped
⅓ cup pine nuts
½ teaspoon salt
½ teaspoon freshly grated
  nutmeg
¼ teaspoon pepper

◆ Cover and cook spinach and water about 10 minutes or until spinach is wilted; drain well. Heat butter in 10-inch skillet over medium-high heat. Sauté garlic in butter. Stir in spinach and remaining ingredients. Cook uncovered over medium heat, stirring frequently, until hot.

Zucchini blossoms are a common sight in Italian markets and are becoming more and more popular in America. Almost all zucchini-flower recipes call for them to be dipped in batter and fried. When buying zucchini blossoms, look for the male blossom —recognizable by its long, soft stem—which is preferred when frying. Female zucchini blossoms mature more quickly and are not as delicious to eat as male blossoms.

CRISP FRIED ZUCCHINI FLOWERS

Fiori di Zucchine Fritti

4 SERVINGS

1 cup all-purpose flour
½ cup dry white wine
½ cup water
1 tablespoon olive oil
¼ teaspoon white pepper
¼ teaspoon freshly grated
  nutmeg
1 egg, separated
8 flat fillets of anchovy in oil,
  cut crosswise in half
16 zucchini blossoms, stems
  removed
Vegetable oil

◆ Mix flour, wine, water, olive oil, white pepper, nutmeg and egg yolk until smooth. Let stand 30 minutes.

Beat egg white in medium bowl until stiff. Fold flour mixture into egg white. Place one fillet of anchovy half inside each zucchini blossom. Heat vegetable oil (1 inch) in deep fryer or Dutch oven to 375°. Dip blossoms into batter. Fry 4 blossoms at a time 2 minutes or until golden brown; drain on paper towels.

VENETIAN ZUCCHINI

Zucchine alla Veneziana

6 SERVINGS

6 medium zucchini, cut into
  julienne strips
1 teaspoon salt
¼ cup olive oil
2 cloves garlic, finely chopped
1 teaspoon freshly grated
  nutmeg
Freshly ground pepper

◆ Spread zucchini on cutting board; sprinkle with salt. Tilt board slightly; let stand 30 minutes.

Heat oil in 12-inch skillet over medium-high heat. Sauté garlic in oil. Rinse zucchini; squeeze and pat dry. Stir zucchini and nutmeg into garlic mixture. Cook uncovered about 5 minutes, stirring frequently, until tender. Sprinkle with pepper.

Crisp Fried Zucchini Flowers

ZUCCHINI WITH FRESH HERBS

Zucchine Speziate

4 SERVINGS

2 medium carrots, cut into
  julienne strips
4 medium zucchini, cut into
  julienne strips
2 tablespoons butter
1 tablespoon chopped fresh
  sage
1 teaspoon chopped fresh dill
  weed
1½ teaspoons lemon juice
¼ teaspoon salt
¼ teaspoon pepper

◆ Place steamer basket in ½ inch water (water should not touch bottom of basket). Place carrots in basket. Cover tightly and heat to boiling; reduce heat. Steam carrots 3 minutes; add zucchini. Steam 4 to 6 minutes or until carrots and zucchini are crisp-tender.

Heat butter in 12-inch skillet over medium heat. Stir in carrots, zucchini and remaining ingredients. Cook uncovered 2 to 3 minutes, stirring gently, until hot.

ASSORTED VEGETABLE CROQUETTES

Ortaggi Fritti

6 SERVINGS

1 small head cauliflower, separated into flowerets
3 tablespoons lemon juice
2 jumbo eggs
1½ cups all-purpose flour
1 teaspoon salt
1 teaspoon pepper
2 small zucchini, cut crosswise
  into ½-inch pieces
1 can (14 ounces) artichoke
  hearts, drained and cut in
  half*
Vegetable oil

◆ Heat cauliflower and enough water to cover to boiling. Cover and boil about 8 minutes or until tender; drain. Mix lemon juice and eggs. Mix flour, salt and pepper. Dip vegetables into egg mixture; coat with flour mixture. Heat oil (1½ inches) in deep fryer or Dutch oven to 375°. Fry a few vegetables at a time 1 to 2 minutes or until golden brown; drain on paper towels.

*1 package (9 ounces) frozen artichoke hearts, thawed and drained, can be substituted for the canned artichoke hearts.

EGGPLANT AND OLIVE SALAD

Contorno di Melanzane e Olive Nere

6 SERVINGS

4 medium eggplant (about 1
    pound each)
⅓ cup salt
1 cup all-purpose flour
Vegetable oil
½ cup olive oil
1 tablespoon chopped fresh
    parsley
1 tablespoon capers, drained
    and chopped
4 flat fillets of anchovy in oil,
    rinsed and chopped
3 cloves garlic, finely chopped
1½ cups imported Italian black
    olives, pitted
Freshly ground pepper

◆ Pare eggplant; cut into 1-inch cubes. Spread eggplant on cutting board; sprinkle with salt. Tilt board slightly; let stand 30 minutes.

Rinse eggplant; pat dry. Coat eggplant with flour. Heat vegetable oil (1 inch) in deep fryer or Dutch oven to 375°. Fry about 8 cubes eggplant at a time 2 minutes or until golden brown; drain on paper towels. Keep warm.

Heat olive oil in 10-inch skillet over medium-high heat. Sauté parsley, capers, fillets of anchovy and garlic in olive oil. Reduce heat to medium; stir in olives. Cook about 5 minutes, stirring frequently, until olives are hot. Toss olive mixture and eggplant; sprinkle with pepper.

Eggplant can have a slightly bitter taste, so it is always an excellent idea to salt the eggplant. When salt touches the eggplant, a chemical reaction draws the inner juices to the surface, and rinsing the eggplant thereafter eliminates its bitterness. In some Italian dishes, eggplant is not salted and rinsed; instead, sugar is added to create a bittersweet flavor.

THREE-COLOR PEPPER SALAD

Peperonata ai Tre Colori

4 SERVINGS

1 cup olive oil
2 cloves garlic, finely chopped
1 small red onion, chopped
2 medium red bell peppers, cut
    into ½-inch strips
2 medium green bell peppers,
    cut into ½-inch strips
2 medium yellow bell peppers,
    cut into ½-inch strips
6 fresh pear-shaped tomatoes,
    peeled and chopped
½ teaspoon salt
¼ teaspoon pepper

◆ Heat oil in 12-inch skillet over medium-high heat. Sauté garlic and onion in oil. Reduce heat to medium-low; stir in bell peppers. Cover and cook 10 minutes or until tender. Remove peppers. Stir tomatoes, salt and pepper into skillet. Cook uncovered about 5 minutes, stirring frequently, until hot.

Remove skin from bell peppers; arrange bell peppers in star shape on large plate. Place tomatoes in center of bell peppers; pour liquid from skillet over top. Serve hot or at room temperature.

Peperonata is the most popular pepper salad in Italy. The colorful red, green and yellow peppers are easier to digest if they are skinned or soaked in milk before cooking. However, if you choose not to remove skins after cooking, your salad will be just as delicious.

PIQUANT SALAD

Insalata Piccante

4 SERVINGS

½ pound fresh green beans
1 head radicchio
1 teaspoon capers, drained
2 small bulbs fennel, cut into
  fourths
1 head Boston lettuce, torn into
  bite-size pieces
1 jar (6 ounces) marinated
  artichoke hearts, drained
½ cup olive oil
2 tablespoons lemon juice
½ teaspoon chopped fresh mint
½ teaspoon chopped fresh sage
½ teaspoon chopped fresh
  oregano
½ teaspoon salt
¼ teaspoon pepper
1 clove garlic, finely chopped

◆ Boil green beans in enough water to cover about 10 minutes or until crisp-tender; drain and cool. Arrange radicchio leaves around edge of large platter. Mix beans, capers, fennel, Boston lettuce and artichoke hearts; place in center of radicchio-lined platter. Mix remaining ingredients; pour over salad.

NEAPOLITAN ACCOMPANYING SALAD

Insalata di Rinforzo alla Napoletana

4 SERVINGS

1 small head cauliflower, separated into flowerets
1 cup imported Italian black
  olives, pitted
2 tablespoons large capers,
  drained
2 flat fillets of anchovy in oil
4 hard-cooked eggs, cut into
  fourths
¼ cup olive oil
1 tablespoon red-wine vinegar
½ teaspoon salt
¼ teaspoon pepper

◆ Heat cauliflower and enough water to cover to boiling. Cover and boil about 5 minutes or until crisp-tender; drain. Cool to room temperature. Place cauliflower in center of large plate; arrange olives, capers, fillets of anchovy and eggs around cauliflower. Mix remaining ingredients; pour over top.

Piquant Salad, Neapolitan Accompanying Salad

MIXED MARINATED VEGETABLES

Marinata Mista

8 SERVINGS

½ cup olive oil
½ cup red-wine vinegar
2 tablespoons lemon juice
2 large bulbs fennel, cut into
 1-inch pieces
1 pound fresh broccoli, separated into flowerets
4 ounces mozzarella cheese,
 cut into ½-inch cubes
1 stick (2½ ounces) pepperoni,
 cut into ½-inch cubes
2 jars (6 ounces each) marinated artichoke hearts,
 drained
1 jar (12 ounces) marinated
 mushrooms, drained
1 jar (10 ounces) imported
 Italian black olives, drained
 and pitted

◆ Mix oil, vinegar and lemon juice. Toss remaining ingredients. Pour oil mixture over vegetable mixture; toss. Cover and refrigerate about 2 hours or until chilled. Toss before serving.

ARTICHOKE SUMMER SALAD

Insalata di Carciofi

6 SERVINGS

2 packages (9 ounces each)
 frozen artichoke hearts
¾ cup olive oil
3 tablespoons balsamic vinegar
1 tablespoon finely chopped flat
 fillets of anchovy in oil
1 teaspoon fennel seed, crushed
¼ teaspoon salt
¼ teaspoon pepper
1 head romaine, torn into bite-
 size pieces
¼ cup chopped fresh parsley
1 tablespoon capers, drained

◆ Cook artichoke hearts as directed on package; drain and cool. Mix oil, vinegar, fillets of anchovy, fennel seed, salt and pepper. Toss artichoke hearts, oil mixture and romaine; sprinkle with parsley and capers.

CHICKEN, SPINACH AND TOMATO SALAD

Insalata di Spinaci e Pollo Tricolore

6 SERVINGS

¼ cup olive oil

1 small onion, chopped (about ¼ cup)

6 skinless, boneless chicken breast halves (about 1½ pounds)

½ cup dry white wine

½ cup olive oil

2 tablespoons lemon juice

2 tablespoons chopped fresh rosemary

2 tablespoons chopped fresh basil

2 tablespoons chopped fresh mint

½ teaspoon salt

¼ teaspoon pepper

1 pound fresh spinach leaves

6 medium tomatoes, sliced

¼ cup freshly grated Parmesan cheese

◆ Heat ¼ cup oil in 12-inch skillet over medium-high heat. Sauté onion in oil. Reduce heat to medium; add chicken breasts. Cook uncovered about 5 minutes, turning frequently, until chicken is brown; add wine. Cover and simmer about 10 minutes or until chicken is done. Cover and refrigerate until cold.

Cut chicken into strips. Mix ½ cup oil, the lemon juice, rosemary, basil, mint, salt and pepper. Arrange one-third of the spinach on large platter; top with one-third of the tomatoes and one-third of the chicken. Repeat twice with remaining spinach, tomatoes and chicken; drizzle with oil mixture. Sprinkle with cheese. Garnish with fresh rosemary, basil or mint leaves if desired.

TOMATO AND POTATO SALAD WITH HERBS

Insalata Estiva alle Erbe

6 SERVINGS

1 pound small red potatoes

5 fresh pear-shaped tomatoes, cut into fourths

½ cup chopped fresh basil

⅓ cup chopped fresh sage

⅓ cup chopped fresh mint

1 small onion, finely chopped (about ¼ cup)

¾ cup extra-virgin olive oil

½ cup wine vinegar

◆ Boil potatoes in enough water to cover about 20 minutes or until tender; drain and cool.

Peel potatoes; cut into ½-inch slices. Mix potatoes, tomatoes, basil, sage, mint and onion. Pour oil and vinegar over potato mixture; toss. Cover and refrigerate about 2 hours, stirring occasionally, until chilled.

WARM TOMATO-AND-OLIVE SALAD

Olive e Pomodori Saltati

6 SERVINGS

1 jar (10 ounces) imported
   Italian black olives, drained
   and pitted
1 jar (10 ounces) imported
   Italian green olives, drained
   and pitted
¼ cup olive oil
2 tablespoons chopped fresh
   parsley
4 cloves garlic, finely chopped
8 tomatoes, cut into eighths
½ teaspoon salt
¼ teaspoon pepper

◆ Cover olives with cold water. Let stand 30 minutes; drain and pat dry.

Heat oil in 10-inch skillet over medium-high heat. Sauté parsley and garlic in oil. Reduce heat to medium; stir in olives. Cook uncovered 3 minutes, stirring frequently. Stir in tomatoes, salt and pepper. Cook 2 minutes, stirring gently, until tomatoes are warm.

TORTELLINI SALAD

Tortellini Freddi

6 TO 8 SERVINGS

1 package (16 ounces) un-
   cooked fresh or dried tortellini
1 package (16 ounces)
   uncooked fresh or dried spinach tortellini
1 tablespoon olive oil
⅔ cup olive oil
¼ cup chopped fresh basil
2 tablespoons freshly grated
   Parmesan cheese
2 tablespoons large capers,
   drained
¼ teaspoon pepper
2 green onions (with tops),
   chopped
2 medium carrots, sliced
2 flat fillets of anchovy in oil,
   chopped
Freshly ground pepper

◆ Cook tortellini as directed on package—except add 1 tablespoon oil to water. Rinse with cold water; drain. Mix remaining ingredients except freshly ground pepper; toss with tortellini. Cover and refrigerate about 2 hours or until chilled. Toss before serving. Serve with freshly ground pepper.

Warm Tomato-and-Olive Salad

MARINATED ROTINI SALAD

Insalata di Rotini Marinata

8 SERVINGS

2 packages (16 ounces each)
   uncooked rotini
1 tablespoon olive oil
½ cup shredded mozzarella
   cheese (2 ounces)
½ cup shredded Cheddar cheese
   (2 ounces)
¼ cup freshly grated Parmesan
   cheese
½ cup sliced imported Italian
   black olives
½ cup sliced green olives
8 ounces Genoa salami, cut
   into ½-inch cubes
1 package (5 ounces) unsliced
   pepperoni, cut into ½-inch
   cubes
1 medium red onion, chopped
½ cup olive oil
¼ cup dry white wine
1 teaspoon red-wine vinegar
½ teaspoon salt
½ teaspoon sugar
½ teaspoon chopped fresh dill
   weed
¼ teaspoon pepper

◆ Cook rotini as directed on package—except add 1 tablespoon oil to water. Rinse with cold water; drain. Mix rotini, cheeses, olives, salami, pepperoni and onion. Mix remaining ingredients. Pour oil mixture over rotini mixture; toss. Cover and refrigerate about 2 hours or until chilled. Toss before serving.

OLIVES

Olives with pits are almost always served in Italy, a custom that comes down to us from ancient Roman times. Pickled olives have been served as a snack or after a meal for thousands of years, and should never be confused with plain canned black olives. Italians linger over their olives, savoring the last taste of the olive on the pit for as long as possible before they have to relinquish the tasty kernel.

Marinated Rotini Salad

CHAPTER NINE

Desserts

*Ricotta-filled Pastries
(page 208), Little Cheese
Tarts (page 211)
Above: Fresco detail from
a church in the Trastevere
section of Rome*

STRAWBERRIES WITH MARSALA SAUCE
Zabaione alle Fragole

6 SERVINGS

1 quart strawberries
2 cups sweet Marsala wine
½ cup sugar
6 jumbo egg yolks

◆ Remove stems from strawberries. Arrange strawberries, stem sides down, in serving dish. Pour 1 cup of the Marsala over strawberries.

Beat sugar and egg yolks in top of double boiler, using wire whisk, until pale yellow and slightly thickened. Pour just enough water into bottom of double boiler so that top of double boiler does not touch water. Heat water over medium heat (do not boil). Place top of double boiler over bottom. Gradually beat remaining Marsala into egg-yolk mixture. Cook, beating constantly, until mixture thickens and coats wire whisk (do not boil). Immediately pour over strawberries and wine.

The ancient Romans were true gourmets during the height of their empire, and often the necessity of disguising food that was no longer fresh spurred them to create delicious sweet-and-sour recipes, or recipes with wine that could preserve fruit. The Marsala Sauce, similar to eggnog, on these strawberries may have had its beginnings as a preservative for fruit. Romans also used eggnog as a drink for convalescents, and it is still very popular as a "strengthening" drink.

FLAMBÉED BANANAS WITH AMARETTO
Banane all'Amaretto Infiammate

4 SERVINGS

4 bananas
2 tablespoons butter
1 tablespoon granulated sugar
1 tablespoon packed brown
  sugar
1 cup whipping (heavy) cream
½ teaspoon ground cinnamon
⅓ cup amaretto

◆ Peel bananas; cut lengthwise in half. Heat butter in 10-inch skillet over medium heat. Cook bananas in butter until brown; turn. Sprinkle sugars around bananas; cook until sugars are melted and bananas are brown. Carefully remove bananas to heatproof serving platter.

Beat whipping cream and cinnamon in chilled medium bowl until stiff. Spoon or pipe whipped cream around bananas. Heat amaretto in skillet until hot. Carefully ignite and pour over bananas. Serve when flame dies out.

Strawberries with Marsala Sauce

Asti Spumante is a sweet
sparkling white wine from
northern Italy that is similar to champagne. Cham-
pagne is a drier sparkling
wine; Asti Spumante, hav-
ing more natural sugars, is
excellent with—and in—
desserts.

ITALIAN FRUIT SALAD
Macedonia di Frutta

8 SERVINGS

1 cup amaretto
½ cup Asti Spumante or dry
   white wine
2 tablespoons sugar
2 tablespoons lemon juice
1 pint strawberries, sliced
1 cup seedless grapes
2 medium unpared eating apples, cored and cut up
2 medium unpared pears, cored
   and cut up
2 medium bananas, sliced
2 fresh figs or kiwifruit, peeled
   and sliced
½ cup Asti Spumante or dry
   white wine

◆ Mix amaretto, ½ cup Asti Spumante, the
sugar and lemon juice in large serving bowl.
Add remaining ingredients except ½ cup Asti
Spumante; toss. Cover and refrigerate at least
1 hour.

Immediately before serving, pour ½ cup Asti
Spumante over fruit; toss. Top each serving
with sherbet if desired.

FLAMBÉED RASPBERRIES
Lamponi alla Fiamma

6 SERVINGS

2 tablespoons butter
1 tablespoon sugar
3 tablespoons orange-flavored
   liqueur
2 tablespoons lemon juice
2 pints fresh raspberries
¼ cup light rum
¼ cup brandy
Vanilla ice cream

◆ Heat butter in 10-inch skillet over medium
heat. Sprinkle sugar over butter. Cook, stirring constantly, until sugar is brown. Stir in
liqueur and lemon juice. Heat to boiling, stirring constantly; boil and stir 1 minute. Gently
stir in raspberries. Pour rum and brandy over
raspberries. Heat over high heat until hot. Carefully ignite. Spoon raspberry mixture over ice
cream when flame dies out.

ROSE PETAL MARMALADE

Marmellata di Rose

ABOUT 2 HALF-PINTS MARMALADE

1 pound Golden Delicious apples (about 3 medium), pared, cored and each cut into eighths
1 cup water
2 teaspoons grated lemon peel
3 tablespoons lemon juice
4 ounces red rose petals, about 1 1/4 cups packed
4 1/2 cups sugar

◆ Mix all ingredients except sugar in 3-quart saucepan. Let stand 30 minutes.

Heat apple mixture over low heat 30 minutes, skimming foam from surface occasionally; drain. Place apple mixture in food processor or in blender; cover and process until smooth. Mix apple mixture and sugar in saucepan. Cook uncovered over low heat, stirring frequently, until sugar is dissolved and mixture coats spoon.

Immediately pour into hot sterilized jars, leaving 1/2-inch headspace. Wipe rim of jars; cover with lid. Store in refrigerator up to 2 months.

RAISIN-PINEAPPLE FLAMBÉED DESSERT

Ananas e Uvetta al Brandy

6 SERVINGS

1 cup brandy
1/2 cup golden raisins
1/4 cup butter
1 pineapple, pared, cored and cut into 6 rings, about 3/4 inch thick
1/2 cup sugar

◆ Pour brandy over raisins. Let stand 30 minutes.

Heat butter in 12-inch skillet over medium heat. Arrange pineapple rings in single layer in skillet. Sprinkle with half of the sugar. Cook uncovered 4 minutes. Turn pineapple; sprinkle with remaining sugar. Add raisins and brandy; push raisins off pineapple into liquid. Heat over high heat until brandy is hot; carefully ignite. Serve when flame dies out.*

*To extinguish flame easily, cover with lid.

There were many recipes using the petals of roses and violets in ancient Italian cuisine, and today flowers are still used, notably in rose flower water and candied violets. Benedictine monks were well known for their liqueurs made from these flowers, and modern rose and violet fragrances are derived from the monks' study of flowers. Be sure to use flowers that have not been sprayed with pesticides. Always purchase flowers from a reliable source and ask if they are acceptable for eating and cooking.

TRADITIONAL ALMOND COOKIES

Amaretti

*ABOUT **4** DOZEN COOKIES*

3 cups slivered almonds, toasted
3 jumbo egg whites
1½ cups granulated sugar
1 teaspoon powdered sugar
1 teaspoon amaretto
Granulated sugar

◆ Heat oven to 300°. Line cookie sheet with cooking parchment paper, or grease and flour cookie sheet.

Place almonds in food processor or blender; cover and process until finely ground but not pastelike.

Beat egg whites on high speed in medium bowl until stiff. Stir in almonds, 1½ cups granulated sugar and the powdered sugar. Stir in amaretto. Drop by rounded teaspoonfuls about 2 inches apart onto cookie sheet; sprinkle with granulated sugar. Bake 20 to 25 minutes or until brown.

SWEET RICOTTA FRITTERS

Frittelle di Ricotta Dolci

*ABOUT **4** DOZEN FRITTERS*

3 cups granulated sugar
16 ounces ricotta cheese
3 cups all-purpose flour
2 cups dry unseasoned bread crumbs
1 teaspoon licorice-flavored liqueur
2 jumbo eggs
2 teaspoons grated lemon peel
Vegetable oil
Powdered sugar

◆ Mix granulated sugar and cheese in medium bowl. Stir in flour, 1 cup of the bread crumbs, the liqueur, eggs and lemon peel. Shape into 1-inch balls; roll in remaining bread crumbs to coat. Flatten each ball to about ½-inch thickness.

Heat oil (1 inch) in deep fryer or Dutch oven to 375°. Fry 6 to 8 fritters at a time about 1½ minutes or until golden brown. Remove with slotted spoon; drain on paper towels. Sprinkle with powdered sugar. Serve warm.

"A little bitter" is the translation of amaretto, the almond liqueur of Saronno, as well as the name of these crunchy cookies. Traditionally, Italians use half bitter almonds and half regular almonds to make these cookies. Bitter almonds are harvested before they are ripe, and cooks sometimes make their own bitter almonds from the inner kernel of peaches and apricots. As bitter almonds are hard to find in America, this recipe uses regular almonds, which give the cookies a slightly different flavor but make a delicious, crisp-textured almond-flavored cookie.

HAZELNUT MERINGUES

Meringhe alla Nocciola

ABOUT *12 SERVINGS*

6 jumbo egg whites
1 teaspoon vanilla
1 teaspoon white vinegar
2 cups granulated sugar
¼ cup powdered sugar
½ cup hazelnuts (filberts)
1 cup whipping (heavy) cream
2 tablespoons powdered sugar
1 teaspoon cocoa

◆ Heat oven to 275°. Grease and flour 2 cookie sheets or line with cooking parchment paper. Beat egg whites, vanilla and vinegar in large bowl on high speed until foamy. Beat in granulated sugar and ¼ cup powdered sugar, 1 tablespoon at a time, until stiff and glossy.

Place egg-white mixture in decorating bag fitted with star or drop-flower tip. Pipe into 2-inch circles (about 24) onto cookie sheet. (If decorating bag is not available, drop mixture by 2 level tablespoons onto cookie sheet and spread into 2-inch circles.) Bake 45 minutes. Turn off oven; leave in oven with door closed 1 hour. Finish cooling meringues at room temperature.

Heat oven to 400°. Bake hazelnuts in ungreased baking pan 5 minutes or until skins begin to crack. Wrap hazelnuts in clean towel; let stand 2 minutes. Rub hazelnuts in towel to remove skins. Chop hazelnuts. Return to baking pan. Bake about 8 minutes until golden brown, stirring occasionally; cool.

Beat whipping cream, 2 tablespoons powdered sugar and the cocoa in chilled medium bowl until stiff. Fold in hazelnuts. Put meringues together in pairs with about 3 tablespoons whipped cream mixture. Refrigerate 2 hours or until firm.

ALMOND-ORANGE CANDY
Sformato d'Arance e Mandorle

12 SERVINGS

10 thick-skinned large oranges
1 cup honey
2¾ cups slivered almonds,
  toasted

◆ Thinly cut peel from oranges in about ½-inch strips, removing only outer orange layer. Trim any excess white membrane. Cut strips crosswise into slivers to yield 3½ cups. Cover orange peel with cold water. Cover and refrigerate 48 hours, draining and covering with fresh cold water every 12 hours; drain.

Cook orange peel and honey in heavy 12-inch skillet over medium heat about 30 minutes, stirring occasionally, until honey is absorbed and mixture is sticky. Stir in almonds until evenly distributed. Spread in shallow 6-cup dish or ungreased round pan, 9 × 1½ inches. Refrigerate about 3 hours or until chilled and firm. Cut into about 2-inch pieces.

CHESTNUT TRUFFLES
Tartufi di Castagne

ABOUT 30 TRUFFLES

Ground chestnuts have been used as an alternative to flour in Italy, a practice that came about in times when the wheat crop failed. The chestnut flavor adds a rich dimension to these unusual truffles.

1 pound chestnuts*
4 cups water
2 cups milk
⅓ cup butter, softened
1 cup sugar
1 tablespoon cocoa
¼ teaspoon vanilla
1 ounce semisweet chocolate,
  grated

◆ Make a shallow crisscross cut on the side of each chestnut with the tip of pointed, sharp knife. Heat chestnuts and water to boiling; reduce heat. Cover and simmer 15 minutes. Remove about one-fourth of the chestnuts at a time from the water. Peel off shell and skin while chestnuts are warm.

Heat chestnuts and milk to boiling; reduce heat slightly. Boil gently uncovered 15 minutes. Remove milk skin from surface; drain chestnuts thoroughly. Place chestnuts in food processor; cover and process until smooth.

Beat butter in medium bowl on high speed until fluffy. Beat in chestnuts, sugar, cocoa and vanilla until smooth paste forms. Shape into 1-inch balls; roll balls in chocolate. Refrigerate at least 1 hour.

*1 can (16 ounces) chestnuts, drained, can be substituted for the fresh chestnuts. Do not make crisscross cut or boil in water.

NOTE: Using a blender for this recipe is not recommended.

AMARETTO CREAM-FILLED CAKE

Zuccotto Ripieno al Liquore

6 SERVINGS

Sponge Cake (page 200)
½ cup hazelnuts (filberts)
¼ cup amaretto
¼ cup light rum
1⅓ cups whipping (heavy) cream
⅓ cup powdered sugar
⅓ cup chopped blanched almonds, toasted
1 ounce unsweetened chocolate, grated

◆ Prepare Sponge Cake. Heat oven to 400°. Bake hazelnuts in ungreased baking pan 5 minutes or until skins begin to crack. Wrap hazelnuts in clean towel; let stand 2 minutes. Rub hazelnuts in towel to remove skins. Chop hazelnuts. Return to baking pan. Bake about 8 minutes until golden brown, stirring occasionally; cool.

Cut 4-inch circle from cake; cut remaining cake into 1-inch pieces. Mix amaretto and rum; sprinkle over cake. Line large bowl with waxed paper; butter waxed paper. Place cake circle on bottom of bowl; line side of bowl with three-fourths of the cake pieces.

Beat whipping cream and powdered sugar in chilled medium bowl until stiff; fold in hazelnuts, almonds and chocolate. Spoon filling into cake-lined bowl; place remaining cake pieces on filling. Cover and refrigerate 2 hours. Invert onto serving plate; remove bowl and waxed paper. Sprinkle with additional grated chocolate if desired.

ENGLISH ''SOUP'' CAKE

Zuppa Inglese

8 SERVINGS

This cake is an Italian variation on the classic English dessert trifle and is extremely popular in Florence. Trifle, no doubt, found its way to Italy by way of the employees that worked in the London branches of Florentine banking houses.

Sponge Cake (below)
½ cup plus 2 tablespoons sugar
2 eggs
3 tablespoons all-purpose flour
2 cups milk
2 ounces unsweetened chocolate, grated
½ cup light rum
½ cup cherry-flavored liqueur

◆ Prepare Sponge Cake. Beat sugar and eggs in 2-quart saucepan. Gradually stir in flour. Heat milk to scalding. Gradually stir into sugar mixture. Cook over low heat 10 minutes, stirring constantly. Stir in chocolate. Cook 2 minutes, stirring constantly, until chocolate is melted. Cover and refrigerate until cool.

Mix rum and liqueur; sprinkle over cake. Cut cake crosswise into 4 rectangles, 9 × 3¼ inches. Place one cake rectangle in ungreased loaf pan, 9 × 5 × 3 inches. Spread with one-fourth of the filling. Repeat layering 3 times. Cover and refrigerate at least 2 hours.

Sponge Cake

1 tablespoon plus 1 teaspoon sugar
1 tablespoon all-purpose flour
3 jumbo eggs
½ cup sugar
¾ cup all-purpose flour
½ teaspoon salt

Heat oven to 325°. Grease rectangular pan, 13 × 9 × 2 inches. Line bottom with waxed paper; grease waxed paper. Mix 1 tablespoon plus 1 teaspoon sugar and 1 tablespoon flour. Coat pan with sugar mixture.

Beat eggs on high speed in medium bowl 5 minutes or until thickened. Gradually beat in ½ cup sugar. Mix ¾ cup flour and the salt. Fold into egg mixture. Pour into pan.

Bake about 20 minutes or until wooden pick inserted in center comes out clean. Cool 5 minutes. Invert on heatproof surface; remove waxed paper. Cool cake completely.

COFFEE-LAYERED CAKE

Torta al Caffè

12 SERVINGS

4 jumbo egg yolks
½ cup granulated sugar
½ cup milk
1 cup butter, softened
2 cups powdered sugar
2 packages (7.05 ounces each) imported butter biscuits
1 cup cold espresso or very strong coffee
2 tablespoons cocoa
12 maraschino cherries

◆ Beat egg yolks and granulated sugar in 2-quart saucepan on medium speed 30 seconds or until well blended; beat in milk. Heat to boiling over medium heat, stirring constantly. Reduce heat to low; boil and stir 1 minute. Place plastic wrap or waxed paper directly onto milk mixture in saucepan. Refrigerate about 2 hours or until cool.

Beat butter in medium bowl on high speed about 5 minutes or until light and fluffy. Gradually beat in powdered sugar; fold in egg mixture. Dip one-third of the biscuits in espresso (do not soak). Arrange in single layer in ungreased rectangular pan, 13 × 9 × 2 inches. Spread one-third of the filling over biscuits; sprinkle with 2 teaspoons of the cocoa. Repeat 2 times. Cover and refrigerate at least 3 hours. Garnish with cherries.

Statue in the
Bomarzo
Gardens,
near Rome

SICILIAN FROZEN LAYERED CAKE

Cassata Siciliana

6 SERVINGS

1 cup Coffee and Chocolate Ice Cream, softened (page 214)
1 cup Neapolitan Ice Cream, softened (page 213)
Sponge Cake (page 200)
½ cup light rum
½ cup chopped candied fruit or golden raisins
⅓ cup whipping (heavy) cream
1 tablespoon powdered sugar

◆ Place loaf pan, 8½ × 4½ × 2½ inches, in freezer. Prepare Coffee and Chocolate Ice Cream, Neapolitan Ice Cream and Sponge Cake. Pour rum over candied fruit. Let stand 1 hour. Drain, reserving rum.

Cut a rectangle to fit loaf pan, 8½ × 4½ inches, from one end of cake. (Wrap and freeze remaining cake for another use.) Pour reserved rum over cake.

Remove loaf pan from freezer. Spread Coffee and Chocolate Ice Cream in pan and freeze until firm. Spread Neapolitan Ice Cream over ice cream in pan and freeze until firm. Beat whipping cream and powdered sugar in chilled bowl on high speed until stiff; fold in candied fruit. Spread whipping cream mixture over ice cream in pan; top with rum-soaked cake.

Cover and freeze about 8 hours or until firm. Loosen edges with knife; unmold.

ALMOND TORTE FROM PIEDMONT

Torta Alpina Piemontese

6 SERVINGS

2½ cups all-purpose flour
1 cup sugar
2 teaspoons baking powder
1 teaspoon salt
1½ cups finely chopped almonds, toasted
½ cup butter, softened
2 teaspoons almond extract
1 teaspoon vanilla
2 eggs
1 tablespoon sugar

◆ Heat oven to 350°. Grease round pan, 9 × 1½ inches. Mix flour, 1 cup sugar, the baking powder and salt in medium bowl. Stir in remaining ingredients except 1 tablespoon sugar until stiff dough forms. (Dough will be slightly crumbly.) Shape into 1-inch balls. Place in pan. Sprinkle with 1 tablespoon sugar. Bake about 30 minutes or until golden brown.

Sicilian Frozen Layered Cake

"LIFT-ME-UP" DESSERT

Tira Mi Su

8 SERVINGS

4 jumbo egg yolks
½ cup sugar
½ cup milk
16 ounces ricotta cheese
2 ounces semisweet chocolate, grated
2 cups whipping (heavy) cream
2 tablespoons cocoa
1 cup cold espresso or very strong coffee
¼ cup light rum
22 ladyfingers, 4 × 1 × ½ inch
Cocoa

◆ Beat egg yolks and sugar in 2-quart saucepan on medium speed about 30 seconds or until well blended. Beat in milk. Heat to boiling over medium heat, stirring constantly. Reduce heat to low; boil and stir 1 minute. Place plastic wrap or waxed paper directly onto milk mixture in saucepan. Refrigerate about 2 hours or until cool.

Mix milk mixture, cheese and chocolate. Beat whipping cream and 2 tablespoons cocoa in chilled medium bowl until stiff. Mix espresso and rum.

Dip half of the ladyfingers in espresso mixture (do not soak). Arrange in single layer in ungreased rectangular baking dish, 11 × 7 × 1½ inches. Spread half of the cheese mixture over ladyfingers. Spread half of the whipped cream mixture over cheese mixture. Repeat with remaining ladyfingers, cheese mixture and whipped cream mixture. Sprinkle with cocoa. Cover and refrigerate at least 3 hours.

"Lift-Me-Up" Dessert takes its name from the restorative properties of the ingredients included in this dessert. The cream, egg yolks and cheese were thought to be excellent for people in poor health. The addition of rum and espresso are sure to give a lift to those in the best of health! A good quality cream cheese or Mascarpone can be substituted for the ricotta.

SUNDAY CAKE WITH RAISINS

Torta Domenicale

16 SERVINGS

3 tablespoons light rum
3 tablespoons raisins
3 tablespoons golden raisins
3 packages active dry yeast
1/4 cup warm water (105° to 115°)
3/4 cup warm milk (105° to 115°)
6 1/2 to 7 cups all-purpose flour
1 cup sugar
1/4 cup plus 2 tablespoons butter, softened
5 eggs
2 egg yolks
3 tablespoons whipping (heavy) cream
2 teaspoons grated lemon peel
2 tablespoons slivered almonds
Powdered sugar

◆ Sprinkle rum over raisins. Let stand 30 minutes. Drain and discard rum.

Dissolve yeast in warm water in large bowl (mixture will be thick); stir in warm milk. Stir in 1 1/2 cups of the flour and 1 tablespoon of the sugar. Beat until smooth. Cover and let rest 15 minutes.

Beat butter and remaining sugar in large bowl until fluffy. Beat eggs, egg yolks, whipping cream and lemon peel until foamy. Beat egg mixture into butter mixture (mixture will appear slightly curdled).

Stir raisins, egg mixture, almonds and enough remaining flour into yeast mixture to make dough easy to handle. Knead 10 to 12 minutes or until elastic.

Place oven rack in lowest position of oven. Heat oven to 350°. Grease and flour 12-cup bundt cake pan or tube pan, 10 × 4 inches. Place dough in pan. Cover and let rise in warm place 15 minutes. Bake 45 to 50 minutes or until deep golden brown. Invert onto heatproof serving plate. Sprinkle with powdered sugar; cool completely.

Citrus fruits are very important in Italian cuisine, especially in making pastry. When a recipe calls for grated orange or lemon peel, use a grater or small shredder, and be sure to grate no deeper than the colored zest, where the flavor of the peel is concentrated. Avoid the bitter white pith under the skin.

RICOTTA CHEESECAKE WITH CHOCOLATE

Torta di Ricotta al Cioccolato

8 SERVINGS

1 tablespoon sugar
1 tablespoon dry unseasoned
 bread crumbs
16 ounces ricotta cheese
1/2 cup sugar
2 teaspoons grated lemon peel
4 jumbo egg yolks
1/2 cup all-purpose flour
1/2 cup finely chopped candied
 fruit
1 1/2 ounces semisweet chocolate, grated
2 jumbo egg whites

◆ Heat oven to 350°. Grease round pan, 9 × 1 1/2 inches. Mix 1 tablespoon sugar and the bread crumbs. Coat pan with sugar mixture. Mix cheese, 1/2 cup sugar and the lemon peel in medium bowl. Stir in egg yolks, one at a time. Stir in flour, candied fruit and chocolate. Beat egg whites on high speed in medium bowl until stiff. Fold cheese mixture into egg whites. Pour into pan.

Bake about 45 minutes or until set and edge is light brown. Refrigerate until cool. Loosen edge; remove cake from pan. Cover and refrigerate until chilled. Garnish with whipped cream if desired.

STRAWBERRY RISOTTO

Risotto di Fragole

4 SERVINGS

1 cup strawberries, hulled
1/2 cup dry white wine
1/4 cup butter
1 small onion, finely chopped
 (about 1/4 cup)
1 1/2 cups uncooked Arborio rice
4 cups Chicken Broth (page 17)
1/4 cup whipping (heavy) cream

◆ Cut strawberries into fourths. Pour wine over strawberries. Let stand 10 minutes.

Heat butter in 3-quart saucepan over medium-high heat. Sauté onion in butter. Drain strawberries and reserve wine. Reserve 1/2 cup of the strawberries. Stir remaining strawberries into onion mixture. Cook uncovered over low heat, stirring frequently, until strawberries are softened, about 15 minutes.

Stir in rice. Cook, stirring constantly, until liquid is absorbed. Pour 1/2 cup of the Chicken Broth over rice. Cook uncovered, stirring frequently, until liquid is absorbed. Repeat with remaining broth, 1/2 cup at a time. Stir in wine. Cook until wine is evaporated. Stir in whipping cream and reserved strawberries until well blended.

In northern Italy it is common to find polenta cakes and sweet risotto dishes, a reflection of how popular corn and rice are in that region. This strawberry risotto is delicate and refreshing, a perfect summer dessert that is popular in the area around Venice.

Ricotta Cheesecake with Chocolate

FLORENTINE CHOCOLATE PROFITEROLE

Bongo Bongo Fiorentino

6 SERVINGS

1 cup water
¼ cup butter
½ teaspoon salt
1 cup all-purpose flour
4 jumbo eggs
1 cup whipping (heavy) cream
2 tablespoons powdered sugar
½ teaspoon freshly grated
    nutmeg
4 ounces semisweet chocolate
2 tablespoons water
1 tablespoon honey

◆ Heat oven to 400°. Grease and flour cookie sheet. Heat 1 cup water, the butter and salt to rolling boil in 2½-quart saucepan. Stir in flour. Stir vigorously over low heat about 1 minute or until mixture forms a ball. Remove from heat; cool 5 minutes. Beat in eggs, one at a time, until smooth.

Drop by rounded tablespoonfuls about 2 inches apart onto cookie sheet. Bake about 30 minutes or until puffed and golden brown; cool. Cut off tops; reserve. Pull out any filaments of soft dough.

Beat whipping cream, powdered sugar and nutmeg in chilled medium bowl until stiff. Fill puffs with whipped cream mixture; replace tops. Mound puffs on large serving plate. Heat remaining ingredients over low heat until smooth; drizzle over puffs. Freeze 2 hours or until the dessert is firm.

RICOTTA-FILLED PASTRIES

Cannoli di Ricotta

12 PASTRIES

1 cup powdered sugar
16 ounces ricotta cheese
½ cup slivered almonds, toasted
⅓ cup miniature semisweet chocolate chips
1 tablespoon amaretto
12 cannoli pastry shells
12 maraschino cherries, cut in half
1 tablespoon powdered sugar
1 tablespoon cocoa

◆ Gradually stir powdered sugar into cheese; stir in almonds, chocolate chips and amaretto. Carefully spoon filling into pastry shells, filling from the center out. Place cherry half in filling on both ends of each shell. Mix 1 tablespoon powdered sugar and the cocoa; sprinkle over shells.

Florentine Chocolate
Profiterole

ITALIAN APPLE PIE

Crostata di Mele

6 SERVINGS

Tart Dough (page 211)
6 medium cooking apples, pared
  and thinly sliced
2 tablespoons lemon juice
2 tablespoons sugar

◆ Prepare Tart Dough. Heat oven to 375°. Toss apples and lemon juice. Roll three-fourths of the dough into 11-inch circle on lightly floured surface. Ease dough into ungreased pie plate, 9 × 1¼ inches, pressing firmly against bottom and side. Turn apples into pie plate; sprinkle with sugar.

Roll remaining dough into rectangle, 11 × 5 inches; cut lengthwise into 10 strips, ½ inch wide. Arrange strips in lattice pattern on apples. Fold edge of lower crust over ends of strips. Seal and flute. Bake 30 to 35 minutes or until crust is golden brown.

SWEET CINNAMON FETTUCCINE

Fettuccine Dolci alla Cannella

4 SERVINGS

2 cups all-purpose flour
2 jumbo eggs
1 tablespoon sugar
1 teaspoon ground cinnamon
1 teaspoon grated lemon peel
Vegetable oil

◆ Place flour in a mound on surface or in large bowl. Make a well in center of flour; add remaining ingredients except oil. Mix thoroughly with fork, gradually bringing flour to center, until dough forms. (If dough is too sticky, gradually add flour when kneading. If dough is too dry, mix in water.) Knead on lightly floured surface about 10 minutes or until smooth. Cover with plastic wrap or aluminum foil. Let stand 15 minutes.

Divide dough into 4 equal parts. Roll and cut each part into fettuccine as directed in Egg Noodles (page 36).

Heat oil (2 inches) in deep fryer or 4-quart Dutch oven to 375°. Fry a few noodles at a time about 30 seconds or until golden brown; drain on paper towels. Keep noodles warm in 200° oven. Serve warm.

LITTLE CHEESE TARTS

Tartine al Formaggio

16 TARTS

Tart Dough (below)
1/3 cup golden raisins
2 tablespoons amaretto or rum
16 ounces ricotta cheese
1/2 cup sugar
2 teaspoons grated lemon peel
4 jumbo egg yolks
1/2 cup all-purpose flour
1/2 cup finely chopped candied
    fruit
2 jumbo egg whites

◆ Prepare Tart Dough. Mix raisins and amaretto. Let stand 30 minutes.

Heat oven to 400°. Mix cheese, sugar and lemon peel. Stir in egg yolks, one at a time. Stir in raisin mixture, flour and candied fruit. Beat egg whites in medium bowl on high speed until stiff. Fold cheese mixture into egg whites.

Roll dough 1/8 inch thick on lightly floured surface; cut into sixteen 4-inch circles. Ease dough circles into ungreased 3-inch tart pans or 6-ounce custard cups. Divide cheese mixture evenly among tart pans (about 1/4 cup each). Bake 20 to 25 minutes or until crust is golden brown and filling is set. Serve warm or cold. Sprinkle with powdered sugar if desired. Immediately refrigerate any remaining tarts.

Tart Dough

2 cups plus 2 tablespoons all-
    purpose flour
1/2 cup sugar
1/2 cup plus 2 tablespoons but-
    ter, softened
2 teaspoons grated lemon peel
1/2 teaspoon salt
1 jumbo egg
1 jumbo egg yolk

Mix all ingredients until dough forms. Knead 3 minutes on unfloured surface. Shape into ball. Cover and refrigerate 2 hours or until chilled.

NEAPOLITAN ICE CREAM

Gelato alla Napoletana

I PINT ICE CREAM

1 cup milk
¾ cup sugar
4 jumbo egg yolks
1 cup whipping (heavy) cream
½ cup hazelnuts (filberts)
½ teaspoon cocoa

◆ Mix milk, sugar and egg yolks in 2-quart saucepan. Cook over medium heat, stirring constantly, just until bubbles appear around edge. Cover and refrigerate about 1½ hours or until cool.

Heat oven to 400°. Bake hazelnuts in ungreased baking pan 5 minutes or until skins begin to crack. Wrap hazelnuts in clean towel; let stand 2 minutes. Rub hazelnuts in towel to remove skins. Chop hazelnuts finely. Return to baking pan. Bake about 8 minutes until golden brown, stirring occasionally; cool.

Stir whipping cream, hazelnuts and cocoa into milk mixture. Freeze in ice-cream maker as directed by manufacturer.

ICE-CREAM PARLOR

Procopio Coltelli, a Sicilian, was a master at making ice cream and ices. In the eighteenth century he opened an ice-cream parlor in Paris—Europe's first—and popularized Italian ices. His store was a tradition for roughly 200 years, passed down through generations of the Coltelli family.

Neapolitan Ice Cream, Traditional Almond Cookies (page 196)

AMARETTO ICE CREAM
Gelato all'Amaretto

ABOUT 1 QUART ICE CREAM

½ cup amaretto
½ cup golden raisins
¾ cup sugar
1 cup whole milk
1 jumbo egg
6 Traditional Almond Cookies
   (page 196) or 12 purchased
   Amaretti cookies crushed
   (about ½ cup)
1 cup whipping (heavy) cream
¼ teaspoon salt

◆ Pour amaretto over raisins. Let stand at least 8 hours. Drain, reserving 2 tablespoons amaretto.

Mix sugar, milk and egg in 2-quart saucepan. Cook over medium heat, stirring constantly, just until bubbles appear around edge. Cover and refrigerate about 1½ hours or until cool.

Stir cookies into milk mixture. Beat whipping cream in chilled medium bowl until stiff. Fold milk mixture into whipped cream. Fold in reserved amaretto, the raisins and salt. Freeze in ice-cream maker as directed by manufacturer.

COFFEE AND CHOCOLATE ICE CREAM
Gelato al Caffè e Cioccolato

1 QUART ICE CREAM

¾ cup sugar
1 cup whole milk
1 tablespoon freeze-dried in-
   stant coffee
1 teaspoon cocoa
2 jumbo eggs
1 cup whipping (heavy) cream

◆ Mix all ingredients except whipping cream in 2-quart saucepan. Cook over medium heat, stirring constantly, just until bubbles appear around edge. Cover and refrigerate about 1½ hours or until cool.

Beat whipping cream in chilled medium bowl until soft peaks form. Fold milk mixture into whipped cream. Freeze in ice-cream maker as directed by manufacturer.

ORANGE-LEMON SHERBET

Sorbetto alle Arance e Limone

ABOUT *1* QUART SHERBET

½ cup sugar

1 cup water

1⅔ cups orange juice (about 5 oranges)

¼ cup plus 2 tablespoons lemon juice (about 2 lemons)

3 jumbo egg whites

½ cup sugar

2 tablespoons orange- or cherry-flavored liqueur

◆ Mix ½ cup sugar and the water in 2-quart saucepan; heat to boiling. Boil uncovered about 10 minutes or until thickened and reduced to about ⅓ cup. Remove from heat; stir in orange juice and lemon juice. Cook uncovered over low heat 5 minutes, stirring frequently. Cover and refrigerate about 1½ hours or until cool.

Beat egg whites and ½ cup sugar just until blended; gradually stir in liqueur. Mix juice mixture and egg white mixture. Freeze in ice-cream maker as directed by manufacturer.

MENUS

◆

A SUNDAY TRADITION

Cheese Pillows
Tortellini Soup
Pork Roast with Rosemary
Green Beans with Lemon Butter
Sunday Cake with Raisins

SUGGESTED WINES:
White: *Soave Bolla*
Red: *Bigi Orvieto Dry*

◆

A DO-AHEAD MEAL

Eggplant Appetizer
Baked Lasagne
Veal with Caper Sauce
Mixed Marinated Vegetables
Italian Fruit Salad

SUGGESTED WINES:
Red: *Castello DiAlbola Chianti*
Rosé: *Rosatello Ruffino*

◆

AN EASY FEAST

Basil Toast
Tortellini with Mushroom and Brandy Sauce
Grilled Salmon with Mint Marinade
Almond-Orange Candy

SUGGESTED WINES:
White: *EST! EST! EST! Di Montefiascone*
Red: *Corvo Di Salaparuta*

◆

QUICK AND EASY DINNER

Shrimp with Prosciutto
Egg Drop Soup
Peas and Basil Omelet
Flambéed Raspberries

SUGGESTED WINES:
White: *Verdicchio Di Iesi, Fazi, Battaglia*
Red: *Rosso Brolio, Ricasoli*

◆

A WARMING WINTER MEAL

Spicy Eggplant
Homemade Minestrone
Rustic Pizza Pie
Almond Torte from Piedmont

SUGGESTED WINES:
White: *Vernaccia di San Gimignano (Melini)*
Red: *Valpolicella Ruffino*

◆

A CASUAL DINNER

Spicy Meatballs
Spaghetti of the Night
Chicken Breasts in Lemon-Caper Sauce
Fresh Peas and Prosciutto
Coffee and Chocolate Ice Cream

SUGGESTED WINES:
White: *Pinot Grigio, Volpe Pasini*
Red: *Inferno, Negri*

◆

NORTHERN ITALIAN FEAST

Baked Fennel
Risotto with Gorgonzola Cheese
Braised Veal Roast
Sweet Ricotta Fritters

SUGGESTED WINES:
White: *Pinot Grigio, Volpe Pasini*
Red: *Inferno, Negri*

◆

FROM THE ITALIAN RIVIERA

Stuffed Mussels
Linguine with Clam Sauce
Fillet of Sole, Parma-style
Piquant Salad
Orange-Lemon Sherbet

SUGGESTED WINES:
White: *Bianco Brolio Antinori*
Red: *Vino Nobile di Montepulciano, "Fassati"*

◆

EXOTIC SOUTHERN ITALIAN MEAL

Eggplant Appetizer
Half-shell Noodles with Broccoli and Ricotta Sauce
Fresh Tuna and Peas
Traditional Almond Cookies

SUGGESTED WINES:
White: *Galestro, Ruffino*
Red: *Barbaresco, Bersano*

◆

A REFRESHING SUMMER DINNER

Savory Tomato Appetizer
Summer Cold Soup
Grilled Swordfish
Tomato and Potato Salad with Herbs
Ricotta-filled Pastries

SUGGESTED WINES:
White: *Tocai Friulano, Collio*
Red: *Lambrusco, Riunite*

◆

Following pages: Menu for a Do-Ahead Meal: (Clockwise from upper left) Italian Fruit Salad (page 194), Mixed Marinated Vegetables (page 184), Veal with Caper Sauce (page 145), Baked Lasagne (page 50), Eggplant Appetizer (page 2)

Canadian Metric Conversion Tables

Dry and Liquid Measurements

IMPERIAL	METRIC
¼ teaspoon	1 mL
½ teaspoon	2 mL
1 teaspoon	5 mL
1 tablespoon	15 mL
2 tablespoons	25 mL
3 tablespoons	50 mL
¼ cup	50 mL
⅓ cup	75 mL
½ cup	125 mL
⅔ cup	150 mL
¾ cup	175 mL
1 cup	250 mL

Temperatures

FAHRENHEIT	CELSIUS
32°F	0°C
212°F	100°C
250°F	121°C
275°F	140°C
300°F	150°C
325°F	160°C
350°F	180°C
375°F	190°C
400°F	200°C
425°F	220°C
450°F	230°C
475°F	240°C

Common Cooking & Baking Utensil Equivalents

BAKEWARE	IMPERIAL	METRIC
Round Pan	8 × 1½ inches	20 × 4 cm
	9 × 1½ inches	22 × 4 cm
Square Pan	8 × 8 × 2 inches	22 × 22 × 5 cm
	9 × 9 × 2 inches	23 × 23 × 5 cm
Baking Dishes	11 × 7 × 1½ inches	28 × 18 × 4 cm
	12 × 7½ × 2 inches	30 × 19 × 5 cm
	13 × 9 × 2 inches	33 × 23 × 5 cm
Loaf Pan	8½ × 4½ × 2½ inches	22 × 11 × 6 cm
	9 × 5 × 3 inches	23 × 13 × 8 cm
Tube Pan	10 × 4 inches	25 × 10 cm
Jelly Roll Pan	15½ × 10½ × 1 inch	39 × 27 × 2.5 cm
Pie Plate	9 × 1¼ inches	23 × 3.2 cm
	10 × 1½ inches	25 × 4 cm
Muffin Cups	2½ × 1¼ inches	6 × 3.2 cm
	3 × 1½ inches	8 × 4 cm
Skillet	10 inches	25 cm
Casseroles and Saucepans	1 quart	1 L
	1½ quarts	1.5 L
	2 quarts	2 L
	2½ quarts	2.5 L
	3 quarts	3 L
	4 quarts	4 L

Note: The recipes in this cookbook have not been developed or tested in Canadian metric measures. When converting to Canadian metric, some variations in recipe quality may be noted.

INDEX

◆

CREDITS

—◆—

Prentice Hall Press

Vice-President and Publisher: Anne M. Zeman
Senior Editor: Rebecca W. Atwater
Editor: Anne Ficklen
Editorial Assistant: Rachel Simon
Assistant Art Director, Design: Patricia Fabricant
Assistant Art Director, Photography: Frederick J. Latasa
Prop Styling: IDESIGN
Illustrator: Laurie Lee Davis
Production Managers: Ellen Kagan, Lessley Davis
Production Editor: Peter Katucki

General Mills, Inc.

Editor: Lois Tlusty
Test Kitchen Home Economists: Mary H. Johnson, Diane Undis
Recipe Copy Editor: Laurie Long
Administrative Assistant: Phyllis Weinbender
Food Stylists: Cindy Lund, Mary Sethre
Photographer: Ed Vetsch
Photography Assistant: Brian Holman
Director, Betty Crocker Food and Publications Center: Marcia Copeland
Assistant Manager, Publications: Lois Tlusty

75 POINTS

SAVE these Betty Crocker Points and redeem them for big savings on hundreds of kitchen, home, gift and children's items! For catalog, send 50¢ with your name and address to: General Mills, P.O. Box 5389, Mpls., MN 55460.

Redeemable with cash in USA before May 1999. Void where prohibited, taxed or regulated.

S

CUT OUT AND SAVE